YORK

General Editors:
of Stirling) & P
University of B

Somerset Maugham

SELECTED SHORT STORIES

Notes by Peter Kuch
BA (LAMPETER) B LITT (OXON)
Lecturer, Avondale College
New South Wales

LONGMAN
YORK PRESS

YORK PRESS
Immeuble Esseily, Place Riad Solh, Beirut.

LONGMAN GROUP LIMITED
London
*Associated companies, branches and representatives
throughout the world*

© Librairie du Liban 1980

All rights reserved. No part of this publication may be reproduced, stored in a retrieval system, or transmitted in any form or by any means, electronic, mechanical, photocopying, recording, or otherwise, without the prior permission of the copyright owner.

First published 1980
ISBN 0 582 78113 2
Printed in Hong Kong by
Wilture Enterprises (International) Ltd.

Contents

Part 1: Introduction *page* 5
    The life of Somerset Maugham 5
    Biographical summary 18
    A note on the text 18

Part 2: Summaries 19
    Rain 19
    The Pool 24
    Appearance and reality 30
    The Voice of the Turtle 35
    The Unconquered 40

Part 3: Commentary 46
    The short story 46
    Special studies 52

Part 4: Hints for study 70

Part 5: Suggestions for further reading 74

The author of these notes 76

Part 1

Introduction

The life of Somerset Maugham

Somerset Maugham was born the youngest in a family of six boys, four of whom survived, at the British Embassy in Paris on 25 January 1874. His father had travelled extensively in Africa and Asia Minor before being appointed Solicitor to the Embassy in 1850. From one of his trips he brought back an emblem known as the sign against the evil eye, which his son was to use extensively on the spine of all his books. 'My father was a stranger to me when he was alive', Maugham later told his nephew. 'Yet somehow that sign against the evil eye seems to have bound us together.'

Maugham's mother, who was twenty years younger than her husband, suffered from tuberculosis. The doctors of the day had the quaint notion that this could be cured by childbearing. Her first son, Charles Ormond, was born on 14 November 1865; the second, Frederick Herbert, later Lord Chancellor of England, followed on 20 October 1866; and the third son, christened Henry Neville, was born on 12 June 1868.

Paris in the 1880s was fashionable, fascinating, and frivolous. Robert Maugham's career prospered; as well as working for the Embassy he went into private practice. He took a fashionable apartment for his family on the third floor of Number 25, Avenue d'Antin, a broad street lined with chestnut trees on the south side of the Champs-Elysées, close to the elegant heart of the capital. Edith Maugham's sparkling humour attracted many to her salon, which though neither exclusively literary nor brilliant was not undistinguished. Prosper Mérimée, the master of the short novel, and the engraver Gustave Doré called occasionally, as did the radical politician, Georges Clemenceau, later a Prime Minister of France.

The Maughams' family and social life was interrupted by the Franco-Prussian War which broke out in the summer of 1870. They were forced to flee Paris, which eventually fell to the Prussians, and though their apartment escaped unscathed, Robert Maugham's private legal business was ruined. When they returned to Paris in 1871 he was obliged to work harder than ever to re-establish himself and shield his growing family from social and financial decline.

In September 1877, when Maugham was nearly four years old, his three elder brothers were sent to boarding school in England. With his brothers away, and his father working long hours, the lonely young boy turned increasingly to his mother for companionship and love. In the mornings he was allowed to visit her while she rested from her bath, and after lunch, when his nurse brought him back from playing in the Champs-Elysées, he was taken to her rooms to meet the friends who had gathered there for the afternoon.

The sheltered world which Maugham's mother provided for her son was shattered when she died in 1882. Her love, her protection, her beauty, and the elegant pattern of her life were suddenly torn from him. Her death scarred him for life. His father survived his mother by only two and a half years. In 1884 he died of cancer and grief. Though there had been little friendship or understanding between the ten-year-old boy and his sixty-year-old father, Maugham suffered deeply. He was now deprived of both emotional and financial security. When their father's estate was settled the four brothers were shocked to find that their inheritance was much smaller than they had expected. This miscalculation made a deep impression on Maugham, and for the rest of his life he pursued economic security obsessively.

As he was too young to stay by himself in Paris, Maugham was sent to Whitstable in England to board with his uncle and aunt. They were in their mid-fifties and were childless. His uncle, who was the vicar of All Saints, Whitstable, was severe, parsimonious, and pedantic. His aunt, though pleasant, was ineffectual; she was prim and respectable, kindly but straitlaced. Neither was emotionally equipped to perform their new roles. Maugham was greatly relieved when he was sent to the King's School, Canterbury, a few months after his tenth birthday. But if in his foster home he had been largely ignored, he was tormented at school. He was small, spoke English with a pronounced French accent, and stammered badly, which made him a target for the rougher boys.

Maugham's years at the King's School were largely unhappy. When he was sixteen he contracted a lung infection, and his uncle, remembering that the boy's mother had suffered from tuberculosis, sent him to the dry climate of the South of France to convalesce. Here he was happy. The flavour of the joyous, carefree life he was able to lead lingered in his mind, and when he returned to the King's School he begged to be allowed to go abroad again. The following year, 1891, he went to Heidelberg in Germany, and though he did not matriculate into the university, he took advantage of the lectures, the library, the municipal theatre, and the heady discussions with other young people in the cafés and beer-gardens. In Heidelberg he moved closer to the scepticism that he was eventually to embrace. The seeds of scepticism had been sown at Whitstable when God seemed to him to have been indifferent to his stammer. The character of his uncle lessened his respect for religion and fertilised his doubt, and now his new-found freedom abroad brought his unbelief to germination. Religious belief, he concluded, was neither life-enhancing nor necessary.

When he returned to England it was proposed that he enter the Church or the Civil Service. Both were rejected in favour of accountancy, at which he lasted a mere six weeks. To his guardian's relief he suggested that he should study medicine, though at the time he was more attracted to the freedom of living in London than to the idea of becoming a doctor. He entered the medical school attached to Saint Thomas's Hospital in the autumn of 1892, and studied just hard enough to pass his examinations. Most of his spare time was spent reading English, French, and Italian literature as a preparation for writing. At medical school he wrote plays, which were unproducible, and short stories, which were unpublishable, though the latter must have had some merit, for Fisher Unwin, one of the publishing houses that rejected them, asked him if he had a short novel for their pseudonym series on hand. He immediately sat down and wrote *Liza of Lambeth*, the book that launched him as a writer.

Liza of Lambeth is a slum novel in the manner of George Gissing, Arthur Morrison, and Edwin Pugh, though it makes no overt political or social statements. The book is based on Maugham's experiences from a part of the fourth year of his medical course when he was assigned as an obstetrics clerk to the Lambeth slums. It is set in the close-knit community of Vere Street, Lambeth, and recounts the illicit love of Liza Kemp, a young, single, factory worker and favourite with the Street, and Jim Blakeston, a married man with five children. When their relationship is several months old, Liza is confronted by Jim's wife, who beats her so savagely that she has a miscarriage and dies. The story is told simply and with remarkable restraint, and the style is crisp and clear.

The publication of *Liza of Lambeth* created a minor public fuss and a major private upheaval. It was condemned as 'dirty' by a number of literary magazines, and denounced from the pulpit of Westminster Abbey. Maugham was delighted. Against the advice of his relatives and publishers he threw up his medical career, though he had recently qualified, and went to Spain. There he wrote a callow eulogy of Andalusia, which remained unpublished until 1905, and an autobiographical novel, *The Artistic Temperament of Stephen Carey*, which was rejected by several publishers before being abandoned. For this Maugham was subsequently grateful; he later used the material to advantage in his best novel, *Of Human Bondage*. For most of 1898 he moved impecuniously between Seville, Toledo, and Rome, before coming to the realisation that his reputation as a writer was far from secure. In 1889 he returned to London, determined to begin writing in earnest.

The following year he published his first volume of short stories,

Orientations. The six stories are 'orientations to find the literary self', as the title page announces portentously in French, so they are characterised by diversity rather than mastery. Several of them are poorly written, with sentences loaded with adverbs and adjectives. They herald, if not the excellence of his prose style, Maugham's unconventionality. He refused to authorise their inclusion in later collections of his work, and did not resume short story writing for almost another twenty years.

Like many young writers Maugham looked to the novel to establish himself as a writer. The seven novels he wrote between 1898 and 1908 are obviously aimed at the popular market. He tried an historical romance set in Renaissance Italy, *The Making of a Saint* (1898); a novel about the Boer War and a young man's loss of faith, *The Hero* (1901); a novel after the style of Wells, Galsworthy, and Bennett on class conflict in marriage, *Mrs Craddock* (1902); an experimental *fin de siècle* novel, *The Merry-Go-Round* (1904); an Edwardian period piece, *The Bishop's Apron* (1906); an Empire novel, *The Explorer* (1907); and a novel about magic and the black arts, *The Magician* (1908), based on Aleister Crowley, whom Maugham had met when he lived in Paris during 1903 and 1904. Of these *Mrs Craddock* is the only novel of merit. It describes the sexually, intellectually, and socially incompatible marriage of a middle-class woman, Bertha Ley, to an ordinary farmer. His penetrating analysis of Bertha's passionate nature anticipates much in D.H. Lawrence, and is undoubtedly one of the better studies of women in modern literature.

The success which Maugham had been striving for eventually came to him as a dramatist. While he had been publishing novels he had also been writing plays, but he was unable to get any of them performed. In October 1907 his luck changed, and the manager of the Court Theatre accepted *Lady Frederick*, one of his comedies of manners. It was a huge success, running for eighteen months to packed houses. Within a short time three more of his plays were also being staged in London. With four plays running simultaneously in the West End, Maugham was assured of celebrity and wealth. From 1908 to 1911 he continued to entertain audiences on both sides of the Atlantic with light comedy. His success enabled him to travel, and to buy a Georgian house at 6 Chesterfield Street in Mayfair.

By 1911 Maugham longed to escape from the theatre and write the autobiographical novel that was pressing itself upon him. 'I was but just firmly established as a popular playwright', he later wrote in *The Summing Up*:

> when I began to be obsessed by the teeming memories of my past life. The loss of my mother and then the break-up of my home, the wretchedness of my first years at school for which my French childhood had so ill-prepared me and which my stammering made

so difficult, the delight of those easy, monotonous, and exciting days in Heidelberg, when I first entered upon the intellectual life, the irksomeness of my few years at the hospital and the thrill of London; it all came back to me so pressingly, in my sleep, on my walks, when I was rehearsing plays, when I was at a party, it became such a burden to me that I made up my mind that I could only regain my peace by writing it all down in the form of a novel. (pp. 126–7)

Maugham disembarrassed himself of these experiences in *Of Human Bondage*. The novel is not simply an autobiography, for fact and fiction have been inextricably mixed. It tells the story of Philip Carey's life from his childhood to his thirtieth year. Philip, a quiet, sensitive boy, an only child, has a club foot. Like Maugham he is orphaned at an early age and sent to live with his aunt and uncle at the vicarage in Blackstable. At school his club foot excites the ridicule of the other boys. He becomes defensive and withdrawn. In his final year he goes to Heidelberg, where he begins to call his religious beliefs and his view of life into question. On his return he has a grotesque love affair with a middle-aged friend of the family. His uncle and aunt plan an ecclesiastical career for him, but he rebels and goes to Paris where he studies painting until he realises that he is devoid of genius. He returns to London to study medicine, where he becomes the victim of a consuming passion for a feckless waitress. It is not until he has experienced a term of grinding poverty as an articled clerk and a shop assistant, and received an inheritance that permits him to complete his medical studies, that he is able to control his passion for her. He finally settles for the uneventful, obscure life of a country doctor, and for being the husband of a pleasant, self-contained girl, considerably younger than himself, whom he loves but is not in love with. Though unhappy and maladjusted, his life progresses towards a philosophy that enables him to face its disappointments and his deformity with equanimity.

Maugham took the title of his novel from the fourth part of Spinoza's *Ethics*, 'Of Human Bondage or the Strength of the Emotions'. He was impressed by Spinoza's assertion that we are in bondage in as far as what happens to us is determined by internal flaws and external circumstances, and that we are free in as much as we are self-determined. In the novel Philip frees himself from the bondages of religion, passion, class-prejudice, art, ambition, and the natural human desire to discover meaning and order in the universe. By the end of the book he has achieved a measure of emotional balance and detachment, the stance at which Maugham himself had arrived by the time he had completed it. Maugham's subsequent books are largely written from the point of view which Philip attains. The narrator of *The Moon and Sixpence* (1919), *Cakes and Ale* (1930), and the short stories is like Philip in that he is experienced, worldly, elaborately self-effacing, and obviously more interested in observing life than in participating in it. After *Of Human Bondage* Maugham is conspicuously in retreat; except for parts of *Cakes and Ale* he never again exposes himself to the same extent.

Many have found the conclusion to *Of Human Bondage* unsatisfactory. How could Philip marry as he does? In *The Summing Up* Maugham admits that he allowed himself to be swayed by other than artistic considerations when he wrote the ending:

> I sought freedom and thought I could find it in marriage. I conceived these notions when I was still at work on *Of Human Bondage*, and turning my wishes into fiction, as writers will, towards the end of it I drew a picture of the marriage I should have liked to make. Readers on the whole have found it the least satisfactory part of my book. (pp.128–9)

What his readers found unsatisfactory in fiction, Maugham found unsatisfactory in life. In 1916 he married Syrie Wellcome, the daughter of the famous philanthropist Dr Thomas Barnardo, and the former wife of the noted scientist Henry (later Sir Henry) Wellcome. They had one child, a daughter, Elizabeth, named after the heroine of Maugham's first novel. The marriage broke up after only eleven years because of the obvious incompatibility of their temperaments, and because of Maugham's ambiguous relationship with Gerald Haxton, a debonair young American he had met in the early months of the First World War when he was serving with a Red Cross Unit in France.

Maugham's twenty-five-year association with this riotous, good-looking young man scandalised many and alienated some. Haxton was energetic, sociable and pleasant, but he drank heavily, had dubious morals, and was a compulsive gambler. In 1916, following an incident in the Covent Garden Hotel in London, he was declared an undesirable alien and forbidden to re-enter Britain. Maugham promptly hired him as a secretary, and took him to the South Pacific where he wanted to do some research for his next novel.

Apart from this trip to the Pacific, Maugham spent the years from 1916 to 1919 in America and Europe, where he was employed for a time as a spy by Sir William Wiseman, the head of what is now MI6. He was sent first to Switzerland, which he later described in his *Ashenden* stories (1928), and then as Wiseman's chief agent to Russia, where he was given the hopeless task of keeping Russia in the war on the side of the Allies, and preventing the overthrow of Kerensky's government by the revolutionaries. On the whole Maugham found his work as a spy an anticlimax, and he was relieved when the fall of the Kerensky government and ill health forced him to return to England. It was discovered that he was suffering from tuberculosis. He was sent to a sanatorium in Scotland, where he wrote his most amusing farce *Home and Beauty*, a short story set in the hospital where he was being treated, 'Sanatorium', and part of *The Moon and Sixpence*, the novel he had collected material for in the South Pacific and which he finished in America, where he went after he had been cured of his tuberculosis.

The Moon and Sixpence is a study of an artist, Charles Strickland, modelled on Paul Gauguin. It charts his flight from his oppressively middle-class life as a London stockbroker to the artists' quarter of Paris and then to Tahiti, where he finds artistic and sexual freedom before dying of leprosy. It is essentially a study of compulsion. The artist, according to Maugham, must create; he cannot do otherwise. Though contemporary readers would probably look askance at such unabashed romanticism, *The Moon and Sixpence* appealed to the public and the literary critics of the twenties.

The Moon and Sixpence, with its exotic setting, signals a significant change in Maugham's way of living and writing. For the next decade he wrote mainly short stories and books set in the Pacific and the Far East, where he travelled extensively from 1920 to 1925. He visited Malaya, Borneo, Indonesia, Thailand, New Guinea, Samoa, Tahiti, Fiji, Singapore, and China. After his visit to China he wrote *On a Chinese Screen* (1922), a collection of musings, impressions, and pen-sketches of the people he had met and the places he had visited. Whenever he travelled Maugham went not only to accessible sea ports and main tourist centres, but to the sparsely populated interiors, using crude native boats to explore strange rivers, or local guides and transport to penetrate deep into unfrequented areas. Once he was nearly drowned in a Sarawak river by a tidal bore; once he was shot at by bandits; and twice he nearly died from malaria.

What captured his attention most, however, were the Europeans he met who had come to live in this part of the world. On his first trip to the Pacific in 1916 he had observed that the abnormal circumstances in which many Europeans were forced to live heightened their individuality. They became more vivid and more extreme than their counterparts in the centres of civilisation. Wherever he went Maugham took careful notes, and his journals are crowded with pen-portraits, some of a few lines, some of a page and more, which are remarkable for their detail and precision:

> Miss Thompson. Plump, pretty in a coarse fashion, perhaps not more than twenty-seven: she wore a white dress and a large white hat, and long white boots from which her calves, in white cotton stockings, bulged. She had left Iwelei after the raid and was on her way to Apia, where she hoped to get a job in the bar of a hotel. She was brought to the house by the quarter-master, a little, very wrinkled man, indescribably dirty. (*A Writer's Notebook*, p.105)

From this note and several others Maugham composed his most famous story, 'Rain'.

In *The Summing Up* Maugham points out that he preferred to travel extensively rather than exhaustively. As soon as he felt he had exploited what a place had to offer he would move on. He kept travelling until he felt that he could no longer absorb what he saw, that he had used up the store of imaginative energy that was required to give his impressions of the people he had met shape and coherence, then he would return to England or the Continent to sort out his impressions and revitalise his powers of assimilation.

The form which best lent itself to giving artistic shape to the material he gathered was the short story. Only rarely did his travels provide him with a completed story. He generally selected from among his notes a number of characters he felt he could bring together without doing violence to their credibility. A careful note about one of the places he had visited was used as a background, its exotic aspects emphasised to reinforce the conflict of personalities or clash of emotions that formed the plot. The exotic setting made the extreme behaviour of the characters plausible, and the extreme behaviour gave the story a strong line. The first two volumes of stories with Far Eastern and Pacific settings, *The Trembling of a Leaf* (1921), and *The Casuarina Tree* (1926), established Maugham as a short story writer of the first rank.

After six trips to the Far East and one to South America, Maugham felt that he could no longer benefit from travel. He retired to the South of France where he bought a villa on twelve acres of land at Cap Ferrat, a promontory that thrusts itself out into the Mediterranean between Nice and Monte Carlo. Maugham had the villa redecorated to his own taste, a library and a writing room erected on the roof, one of the hilly areas landscaped, a swimming pool built on an upper terrace, and a garden of tropical beauty laid out. He called his new home the 'Villa Mauresque'. It housed the various artefacts he had collected on his travels, an impressive collection of French Impressionists and portraits of famous actors from the eighteenth century. The result was a very comfortable residence which was both elegant and tasteful. Guests invited to the Villa Mauresque included the Kings of Sweden and Thailand, the ex-Queen of Spain, the Duke and Duchess of Windsor, the Aga Khan, Sir Winston Churchill, and a host of famous English and American writers.

In literary terms the years from 1927 to 1930 were particularly fruitful for Maugham. During these years he wrote two of his most sparkling comedies, *The Constant Wife* (1927) and *The Breadwinner* (1930), his favourite travel book, *The Gentleman in the Parlour* (1930), and one of his best novels, *Cakes and Ale* (1930). *Cakes and Ale* is memorable for its portrait of Rosie Gann, one of Maugham's most fully realised women characters. Rosie is sincere, unspoiled, voluptuous, warm, generous, and unashamedly sensual. As Robert Calder has pointed out, she is modelled on the actress Ethelwyn Sylvia Jones whom Maugham knew from 1902 to 1913, and with whom he apparently fell in love around 1912. Maugham told his American friend Garson Kanin he had once proposed to the woman on whom Rosie was modelled, but she had refused him and this had altered the course of his life. The refusal may have prompted him to begin *Of Human Bondage* and to embark on his relationship with Syrie Wellcome. It is significant that he created the character of Rosie the year after he was divorced from Syrie. Through the imaginary person of Rosie he was able to re-live a happy past, and offset the failure of his marriage to Syrie.

Cakes and Ale caused a considerable stir in literary circles when it was published. Maugham was accused of satirising the recently deceased novelist Thomas Hardy in his creation of Edward Driffield, and one of the leading writers and critics of the day, Sir Hugh Walpole, in the character of Alroy Kear. Maugham denied these allegations, but subsequent criticism has proved that in fact the whole novel is a thinly disguised tilt at the literary establishment. As well as Hardy and Walpole, Maugham vented his irony on Mr and Mrs Sidney Colvin, well known London socialites who prided themselves on their salon—as the Barton Traffords; Stephen Philips, a bad poet who was lionised for producing one volume of good verse—as Jasper Gibbons; and Edmund Gosse—as the caustic critic Allgood Newton. The excellence of the novel was obscured by the controversy about identifying the targets of Maugham's satire. *Cakes and Ale* contains vivid descriptions of Victorian provincial life, Edwardian social and literary manners, the Georgian scene, and finally, America in the thirties and forties. The reader is transported from one setting to another without any feeling of dislocation, a tribute to Maugham's consummate mastery of the time shift.

None of the other novels he produced in the thirties equals *Cakes and Ale*. *The Narrow Corner* (1932) is a rather unconvincing account of an English doctor's discovery of Buddhism in the Far East. The central character of *Theatre* (1937), for whom life is one long production, is finely realised, but the supporting cast is at best trivial and at worst unpleasant. *Christmas Holiday* (1939) and *Up at the Villa* (1941) are even less distinguished.

The most interesting book for students of Maugham to come out of the thirties was *The Summing Up* (1938). The book, as the title suggests, is a statement of conclusions. It contains apparently definitive pronouncements on Maugham's life, aspirations, ideas, and work. In one sense it fulfilled the same need that *Of Human Bondage* had fulfilled in 1915; it gave shape to ideas and experiences that had shaped him. While fiction was an effective means of achieving order and coherence in 1915, when he was entering his forties, Maugham felt the need for a more dignified approach when he came to give shape to his fifties and sixties. *The Summing Up* is a collection of seventy-seven short essays about his ideas on literature, art, the theatre, ethics, religion, philosophy, and some of the crucial events in his life. Though Maugham does not lay bare his soul—he was always embarrassed by personal confessions—he unhesitatingly strikes a note of intimacy from the opening paragraph. The whole book, though restrained, is warm-hearted.

The work Maugham produced in the late twenties and thirties is dominated by his short stories. The earlier volumes are as good as the best of *The Trembling of a Leaf* and *The Casuarina Tree*. In the same year that he purchased the Villa Mauresque, Maugham published *Ashenden* (1928), a collection of six long stories and a few anecdotes based on his own experiences in the Intelligence Department in the First World War. The stories are loosely tied together by the presence of Ashenden, a British secret agent. Ashenden is not a typical agent. He never devises any ingenious ploys to trap his enemies, he never overpowers anyone with karate or judo, and he is not a weapons expert. He never cracks an enemy code, penetrates another spy ring, or uncovers a major enemy operation. His gravest concern is that he will be unmasked by the neutral Swiss police and expelled from the country to the embarrassment of himself and his friends. He has a phobia about missing trains, and suffers an acute attack of nerves when one of his colleagues has to murder a Greek agent. Nevertheless his humanity endears him to us, and his personality, his taste, and his foibles sustain our interest. As a number of critics have pointed out, Ashenden was the first anti-hero in espionage literature. His impact has been considerable. He is the precursor of Graham Greene's and Eric Ambler's chief agents, and the source for the principal figures in such recent novels as Len Deighton's *The Ipcress File*, and John Le Carré's *The Spy Who Came in from the Cold*.

The title of Maugham's next volume, *Six Stories told in the First Person Singular* (1931), emphasises his distinctive mode of narration. The stories are recounted by a detached, urbane, and worldly-wise narrator whose principal concern is that his listeners are entertained. The collection has much in common with *The Trembling of a Leaf* and *The Casuarina Tree*, though the stories are set in English country houses, Chelsea, and Rhodes, instead of outstations, Pago-Pago, and Singapore. What they show is that life in the centres of civilisation can be as precarious and intense as it is in the Pacific and the Far East.

In *Ah King* (1933), Maugham's next volume of stories, we are taken back to the Far East. The stories are prefaced with a brief description of a Chinese boy named Ah King whom Maugham hired as a servant for a six-month trip through Borneo, Indo-China, and Thailand. At the end of the trip, when Ah King learned that he was to be paid off, he burst into tears. Maugham was amazed and embarrassed. The title is, of course, ironical. Such devotion to duty, Maugham suggests in his stories, is the exception rather than the rule. Most of the stories turn on a situation in which one of the principal characters' selfishness brings ruin to himself and to others. *Ah King* contains one of Maugham's finest stories, 'The Book Bag'. It tells, with great delicacy, of the incestuous love of an orphaned brother and sister who live alone on an isolated plantation in Malaya. The brother goes to England and gets married. On his return his sister commits suicide; her selfishness wrecks his marriage.

When Ray Long, a successful and rather flamboyant publisher of the twenties read 'The Book Bag' he was so impressed by it that he asked Maugham to write a number of brief stories for the magazine *Cosmopolitan*. Maugham obliged with twenty-nine stories. Some are humorous: the cockney woman who runs a hotel in Asia Minor; the unhappy husband-to-be who forces his fiancée into breaking their engagement by embarking on an endless search for the right house; and the American woman who achieves success in London society by inventing a rugged husband and a frontier past. Some are stark and tragic: the four fellow seamen whose happy friendship is brought to a terrible end by jealousy; the artist who becomes a beggar in Vera Cruz; and the Dutchman who is pursued across the islands of the Pacific by an offended native and finally murdered. In 1936 Maugham collected these stories under the title *Cosmopolitans*.

The reviewer of *Cosmopolitans* for *The Times* took Maugham to task for what he considered was writing to a formula. He called his review, 'The Mixture as Before', a term doctors use for a repeat prescription. Instead of being abashed by this criticism, Maugham adopted it as the title for his next volume of stories, which was published in 1940. If the original prescription had worked, why not the mixture as before? Most of the stories have the customary unexpected ending. One of the best, 'The Facts of Life', tells how a young boy violates each one of his father's precepts when he goes to play in a tennis tournament in Monte Carlo, and how by good luck and good management comes out all the better for his misconduct.

Maugham's last volume, *Creatures of Circumstance* (1947), is largely a collection of stories about people's abilities to control their emotions in adverse situations. In 'The Colonel's Lady' a stuffy, overbearing husband is forced to concede that it would be wise for him to forgive his wife a past love affair which he had never suspected until the poetry it inspired made her a literary celebrity. 'The Unconquered' is

Maugham's only story set in the Second World War. It is a powerful, bleak story of a French girl who is raped by a Nazi soldier. When he discovers that she is going to have his child he falls in love with her, but her fierce hatred of him and of what he represents leads her to drown the child as soon as it is born.

Maugham's own wartime experiences were far less harrowing. In 1940 he was evacuated from the South of France on a small collier that was crowded with over 1300 refugees. An account of this voyage, along with a description of the war-work he did for the French and English governments is included in a book, *Strictly Personal*, that was published in 1942. One of his wartime tasks was to write a novel for the American market explaining the effects of the war on a typical English family. The novel, *The Hour Before the Dawn* (1942), is extremely tedious.

From 1942 to 1946 Maugham lived in America. He spent most of his time at Parker's Ferry, a small house on his publisher's estate in South Carolina. Here he completed his eighteenth novel, *The Razor's Edge* (1944). The title for the novel was taken from the Katha Upanishad: 'the sharp edge of the razor is difficult to pass over: thus the wise say the path of salvation is hard.' Maugham is never at his most convincing when he writes about mysticism. His last two novels, *Then and Now* (1946), an historical novel which shows that the axioms of power politics that Machiavelli formulated in *The Prince* had validity then and have it now, and *Catalina* (1948), a light-hearted account of a Spanish cripple's miraculous cure, make pleasant if undemanding reading.

Catalina was written at the Villa Mauresque, to which Maugham was able to return in 1946. Fortunately nothing of great value had been destroyed, though it had been damaged by successive occupations of German, Italian, French, and British soldiers. Maugham was now looked after by Alan Searle, a new secretary who had joined him following Gerald Haxton's death in 1944. For Maugham's friends, Alan Searle was a welcome relief. He was quiet, unobtrusive, and extremely well organised.

In 1949 Maugham published *A Writer's Notebook*. It is a selection of entries from the fifteen large volumes, the notebooks that he had kept from 1892 to 1944. In many ways it is a tantalising book. There are, for example, no entries for the year 1895, when Maugham was twenty-one, nor for the years 1923 to 1929 when he was preparing some of his best work. Its greatest interest is that it shows the type of raw material Maugham used for some of his travel books and many of his short stories.

For the next ten years Maugham devoted himself mainly to essay writing and criticism. *The Vagrant Mood* (1952) is a collection of essays on subjects as diverse as Kant, The Detective Story, Burke's literary style, and an early seventeenth-century Spanish artist, Zurbarán, whom Maugham felt had been unduly neglected.

Ten Novels and Their Authors (1954) was written to 'induce readers to read the novels' of Maugham's favourite writers. His method of inducement is to tell the story of the novelist's life in the hope that interest in the man will re-awaken interest in the work. There are excellent vignettes of Balzac, Stendhal, Melville, and Emily Brontë, and a lively discussion of the relative merits of Dickens's novels. *Points of View* (1958), like *The Vagrant Mood*, contains some pleasant surprises: a lucid analysis of Goethe's novels, and of the prose of Dr John Tillotson (1630-94), the Archbishop of Canterbury in the reign of William III. The essay on the short story largely assembles what Maugham had written in various places. The debate as to who is the better practitioner of the art, Chekhov or Maupassant, is rejoined, with Chekhov emerging more favourably than usual. Katherine Mansfield is allowed a small but delicate talent, and Henry James is once again taken to task for his triviality. The lack of interest in Kipling is again deplored. Poe's famous advice, given in his review of Hawthorne's *Twice Told Tales*, that the short story should be an original piece of fiction which deals with a single incident and which moves without digression in an even line from exposition to conclusion is once again declared sound. The writer, reaffirms Maugham, should aim to delight. It is therefore fitting that the title of his last book should be *Purely for My Pleasure* (1962), a partly literary and partly pictorial record of his own tastes.

Towards the end of his long life Maugham received an impressive number of honours. In 1952 he was awarded an honorary degree from Oxford. On his eightieth birthday in 1954 he was invested with the Order of the Companions of Honour by Elizabeth II, and he was given a dinner by the Garrick Club. In its long history it has honoured only three other members in this way: Dickens, Thackeray, and Trollope. In 1958, along with Sir Winston Churchill and Dame Edith Sitwell, Maugham was elected a Vice-President of the Royal Society of Literature.

He died on 16 December 1965 at the age of ninety-one. In his lifetime he had written twenty novels, over twenty-five plays, eleven travel books and collections of essays, and over one hundred short stories, which he himself estimated had earned him some £1,350,000 in royalties. From this vast amount of work *Liza of Lambeth*, *Of Human Bondage*, *The Moon and Sixpence*, and *Cakes and Ale* will continue to be read and enjoyed as good novels. Whenever *The Circle* and *The Constant Wife* are revived, they are sure to delight audiences. *The Summing Up* has already been widely acknowledged as one of the best philosophical autobiographies to come out of the first four decades of the twentieth century. It will continue to attract readers with its style and with its lucid insights into the writer's art. Finally, Maugham's reputation will undoubtedly rest on the hundred or so short stories which, as a collection, are unmatched in English literature.

Biographical summary

25 January 1874	Born
1892	Enters medical school
1897	First novel, *Liza of Lambeth*
1899	First volume of short stories, *Orientations*
1907	*Lady Frederick* staged at the Court Theatre
1915	*Of Human Bondage*
1916	First voyage to the Pacific
1921	First major collection of short stories, *The Trembling of a Leaf*
1928	Buys the Villa Mauresque
1930	*Cakes and Ale*
1938	*The Summing Up*
1949	*A Writer's Notebook*
16 December 1965	Dies at the age of ninety-one

A note on the text

The Complete Short Stories was first published in three volumes by William Heinemann, London, 1951. It has since been reprinted by Pan Books as the *Collected Short Stories*.

This guide is based on Volume I of the *Collected Short Stories* published by Pan Books, London, 1975.

Part 2

Summaries
of SOMERSET MAUGHAM'S SHORT STORIES

Rain

SETTING: The town of Pago-Pago on the island of Tutuila, Samoa. The boat on which Maugham and Gerald Haxton were travelling from Los Angeles was quarantined there for several days in November 1916. See *A Writer's Notebook*, pp. 96–8 and 103–4.

CHARACTERS: Dr and Mrs Macphail, a medical doctor and his wife who are on their way to Apia. The Reverend Davidson and his wife, returning missionaries. Miss Thompson, a prostitute who has fled from Iwelei, the red light district of Honolulu. Mr Horn, the owner of the guest house in Pago-Pago. The Governor of the islands of Samoa. See *A Writer's Notebook*, pp. 104–5 and 111–12. Maugham talked once to the missionary and his wife, but not to any of the other characters. The plot is his own invention.

PUBLICATION: The story was first published in *The Smart Set*, an American magazine, and then included in *The Trembling of a Leaf* (1921) under the title 'Miss Thompson'.

SUMMARY OF THE PLOT: 'Rain' opens with Dr and Mrs Macphail's discussion of some missionaries, the Reverend Davidson and his wife, the night before the boat on which they are all travelling is due to dock at Pago-Pago. The day they land it begins to rain. An outbreak of measles forces them to stay in Pago-Pago, so they take rooms in a local boarding house. A few hours after they have unpacked another passenger arrives at the boarding house. The incessant, heavy rain forces everyone to stay indoors, and it soon becomes evident that the new arrival is a prostitute who has fled from Iwelei, the red light district of Honolulu, before it was raided by the police. The Davidsons are outraged, and do everything in their power to have the girl, Sadie Thompson, sent away on the next ship. The days before the ship arrives are days of intense struggle. Sadie is determined to stay on the island, for she knows if she is forced to go to either Australia or America she will be put in prison, and the Reverend Davidson is determined to save her soul before she is sent away. He spends hours and hours ostensibly praying with her. The morning the ship is due he is found floating in the sea with his throat cut. He has committed suicide after attempting to make love to, or making love to, Miss Thompson.

ANALYSIS: The story is a masterpiece. The various threads are cleverly woven together in contrasting and complementary patterns. None of the characters dominates the action, yet they are all sharply defined and are shown to possess the individual traits which make their interaction with one another credible. For example, the Reverend Davidson is described as having 'full', 'sensual' lips, and a tragic appearance:

> His dark eyes, set deep in their sockets, were large and tragic; and his hands with their big, long fingers, were finely shaped; they gave him a look of great strength. But the most striking thing about him was the feeling he gave you of suppressed fire. It was impressive and vaguely troubling. (I.14)

The power of the story comes from its close-knit structure and its restraint. The Reverend Davidson is not merely a narrow-minded fanatic; he is courageous and sincere. Sadie Thompson, though at times nauseatingly gross, is warm and generous. Her mental anguish when she realises that she is powerless to prevent her deportation is genuine, and elicits our sympathy. Dr Macphail, the touchstone of good sense, is kind but ineffectual. His inconclusive interview with the Governor serves to emphasise the remorselessness of the tragedy. The intensity with which the Reverend Davidson pursues his mission is cleverly emphasised by having him quote texts from the Bible which, in the circumstances, are both unnecessarily extreme and absolute.

> Now I shall take the whips with which the Lord Jesus drove the usurers and the money changers out of the Temple of the Most High. (I.29)
> If she fled to the uttermost parts of the earth I should pursue her. (I.29)

Both suggest suppressed sexuality, as does the ambiguous, 'A great mercy has been vouchsafed [given] me. Last night I was privileged to bring a lost soul into the loving arms of Jesus.' (I.42) That the Reverend Davidson sees himself as re-enacting part of the ministry of Jesus Christ is evident from his reading the chapter about the woman taken in adultery to his wife and the Macphails. (I.40) The Freudian overtones of the Reverend Davidson's fall however are heard only once, in his 'hills of Nebraska' dream. Practically none of the conversations between Sadie and the missionary are reproduced, and the potentially most dramatic scenes, when he attempts to make love to her, or makes love to her, the remorse for what he has done, and his suicide are not described at all. The ending is swift; the final lines, Sadie's outburst—'You men! You filthy, dirty pigs! You're all the same, all of you. Pigs! Pigs!' suggests all.

The exotic setting is vividly sketched. It is significant that more emphasis is given to the description of Iwelei than to Pago-Pago. The natives, who at first seem to be suffering from physical diseases (l.13), become, in Doctor Macphail's mind, symbols of ancient corruption. (l.32) The maddening effect of the persistent, drumming rain is cleverly suggested by a few brief sentences.

> It was not like our soft English rain that drops gently to the earth; it was unmerciful and somehow terrible; you felt in it the malignancy of the primitive powers of nature ... It seemed to have a fury of its own. And sometimes you felt that you must scream if it did not stop, and then suddenly you felt powerless, as though your bones had suddenly become soft; and you were miserable and hopeless. (l.29)

The exotic setting, the enervating hot-house atmosphere, the ceaseless, tropical rain, and the calm good sense of Dr Macphail work against one another to make the intensity of Sadie Thompson's and the Reverend Davidson's encounter plausible and dramatic.

NOTES AND GLOSSARY:
(*a*) The two main characters, the Reverend Davidson and Miss Thompson, are not introduced until fairly late in the story.
(*b*) Miss Thompson's speech is richly colloquial.
(*c*) We are introduced to Dr Macphail in the first paragraph. By using his point of view Maugham renders the encounter of the main characters more effective. His calmness balances their violence, and his good sense secures the willing suspension of our disbelief. We feel that we can trust him.
(*d*) By only sketching in the effects of the rain, Maugham makes it a contributing factor rather than the cause. This enhances the credibility of the story.
(*e*) Neither the Reverend Davidson nor Miss Thompson complain about the effects of the rain.

was such a big bug that he could afford to put on frills: was so important that he could afford to adopt a conceited air
make the place so hot for them: make it impossible for them to stay
lava-lava: loin cloth
be able to get a wink of sleep: be able to sleep
her hands itched: she was very eager
a bad job about the measles: unfortunate about the measles
fixed yourself up: made yourself comfortable
the feller's tryin' to soak me a dollar and a half: this man wants to charge me one dollar and fifty cents
to pull that stuff with me: to deceive me
not one bean more: not another cent
a shot of hooch: a glass of whisky

real good rye in that grip: very good whisky in that small bag
looked rather fast: seemed immoral
let things slide: allow things to deteriorate
put many so-called Christians at home to the blush: maintain better standards than many professed Christians in England
he's let abuses creep in: he's failed to maintain standards
to have my work cut out: to face a difficult task
If the tree is rotten it shall be cut down and cast into the flames: a paraphrase of the Bible, Mark 7: 18-19
high tea: an early evening meal
The wind blows at his bidding and the waves toss and rage at his word: a paraphrase of Mark 4: 39-41
an advanced dressing-station: a first aid post near the front line of a battlefield
thoughts travelled back: remembered or recalled to mind
pretty rich: rather wealthy
to mend his ways: to improve his behaviour
went round the beds with him: visited the patients with him
They left cards on the Governor: They called on the Governor and left visiting cards (that is, cards on which were printed their name and address)
Terrible, ain't it, bein' cooped up in a one-horse burg like this?: Terrible, isn't it, being forced to stay in a small town like this?
breaking into a medical conversation: interrupting a conversation about medicine
The police refused to stir: the police refused to act
cutting it rather fine: leaving a very small margin of error
flung out of the room: left the room hurriedly, abruptly
at the top of their lungs: very loudly
stand in that creature's shoes: be that person
with their noses in the air: deliberately ignoring
set their faces to an icy stare: assumed a fixed expression, pretended to ignore
whips with which the Lord Jesus drove the usurers and money-changers out of the Temple of the Most High: a reference to Christ driving the money changers out of the Temple at Jerusalem; see Matthew 21:12, Mark 11:15, Luke 19:45, John 2:14-16
If she fled to the uttermost parts of the earth I should pursue her: allusion to Psalm 139:1-12
He'll wear himself out: He'll exhaust himself
had been at me: has been rebuking me

when all's said and done: finally
are in with one another: are collaborating
get it in for: decide to victimise
gave me Hell: abused me
squirmed in his old ducks: appeared embarrassed
rough customer: uncouth and potentially violent
got their knife into her: are victimising her
getting a bit worked up: becoming agitated
Davidson's up to: Davidson's planning
jumpy: nervous
when you come down to brass tacks he has no backbone: the fact is he has no strength of character
I gotter beat it on the next boat: I must leave on the next boat
You can't kid me: you cannot deceive me
a burg: a small town
I don't look no busher, do I?: I don't look like someone who is used to living in a small country town, do I?
to speak straight from the shoulder: to speak directly, unambiguously
shake me off: avoid me
If that'll suit him: If that will be acceptable
straight stuff: respectable occupation
I can't set down to a thing till I get the dope one way or the other: I will not be able to relax until I know the decision
directly tackled: confronted
it's dashed hard to: it is very unfair to
a bit lit up: a little drunk
back's broad enough to bear a few hard words: resolute enough to withstand criticism
You've got me beat: You have defeated me
'I beat it before they could get me', she gasped. 'If the bulls grab me it's three years for mine.': 'I left before they could catch me', she gasped. 'If the police catch me I will be sent to prison for three years.'
to turn over a new leaf: to change one's way of life, morally, for the better
not know which way to look: felt awkward and embarrassed
I am not worthy to touch the hem of her garment: alluding to John 1:27
my heart doesn't bleed for her: I don't feel sorry for her
Bunkum: exclamation of disgust at insincere talk
the thank offering she places at the feet of our Blessed Lord: a reference to Mark 14:3-9. Some think this was Mary of Magdala, herself once a prostitute
she slopped about her room: she moved about the room in a slovenly manner

He felt he would breathe more freely: He believed he would feel relieved
wearing himself to a shadow: exhausting himself
in a little bunch: in a small group
he'll be absolutely dead: he'll be exhausted
to break the news: to inform, to tell
you can that stuff with me: do not do that to me

The Pool

SETTING: Apia, a town on the island of Upolu in Samoa. Kincardineshire, a county south of Aberdeen in Scotland. Maugham first visited Apia in 1916; see *A Writer's Notebook*, pp.108–9. In 1918 he was sent to a sanatorium in Kincardineshire to receive treatment for tuberculosis; see *The Summing Up*, pp.133–4.

CHARACTERS: (The references are to *A Writer's Notebook*) Chaplin, the owner of the Hotel Metropole (pp.109–10); Lawson, a Scottish bank manager (pp.111); his wife, Ethel, a half-caste; her father, Brevald, a Norwegian (p.112); Miller, a German-American (p.111).

PUBLICATION: *Cosmopolitan*, an American magazine, in November 1920. *The Trembling of a Leaf* (1921).

SUMMARY OF THE PLOT: At the beginning of the story the narrator is drinking cocktails with Chaplin in the bar of his hotel, the Hotel Metropole, in Apia, Samoa. Chaplin introduces him to Lawson, a small, thin Scotsman who is plainly an alcoholic. When Lawson leaves the bar Chaplin tells the narrator that Lawson's alcoholism has been caused by the failure of his marriage to Ethel Brevald, a beautiful half-caste. The narrator is at first repelled by Lawson's drunkenness, but several days later he is able to have a sober conversation with him and he realises that he is not only intelligent and well-read, but that he is desperately homesick for the restaurants and concert-halls of London. He then meets Ethel, whom he is surprised to find unlike most half-castes in that she is beautiful, delicate, and cultured. By now his curiosity is aroused. He learns that several years ago, Lawson, for health reasons, came to Apia to manage the branch office of an English bank. Of an evening he used to go to a nearby pool to bathe. It was usually deserted, but one evening, arriving later than usual, he found it occupied by a beautiful half-caste. She seemed to him to be more like a goddess than a human being. Intoxicated by her beauty and by the mysterious setting of the pool, Lawson becomes infatuated with her. They marry and have a son, which awakens Lawson to the realities of Samoan social attitudes. As a quarter-caste his son will be a second-class citizen. Lawson secretly resolves to return to Scotland, where he believes he will be able to secure a better future for his son and the total possession of his wife, from whom he feels he is beginning to be alienated. He obtains a post in a bank in Kincardineshire. For a time Ethel is happy, but she starts to pine for her native Samoa. To the chagrin of her husband and the astonishment of her neighbours she commences bathing in a nearby pool. One day Lawson returns from the bank to find that she has caught a ship back to Samoa. He sells everything and follows her, only to find that she has become even more inaccessibly native. She refuses to leave her parents' home. He begins to drink heavily to escape from the defeat of his aspirations and the squalor of his surroundings. One day he realises that Ethel is having an affair with another man. He beats her, which prompts her lover, a German-American by the name of Miller, to challenge him in public. Miller knocks Lawson down. In a final conversation with the narrator Lawson flatly acknowledges his humiliation and degradation. With nothing to live for he drowns himself in the pool where he had first met Ethel. His body is recovered by Miller.

ANALYSIS: 'The Pool' is a powerful study of a mixed marriage. As we would expect the conflict between Lawson's and Ethel's cultures is brought into focus by the birth of their first child. He wants the boy to grow up a Scotsman, to be given the chance to go to university and take his place as a respected and respectable member of the community. She hates Scotland, and is content to see her son grow up, as she has, among the native Samoans. Lawson's tragedy is the direct result of his initial failure to foresee this conflict of aspirations. His infatuation with Ethel blinds him to the reality of their incompatible ways of life. As the astute Miller tells the narrator, Lawson would have done better to take Ethel as a mistress, then 'he'd have had the whip hand over her.' (I.149) This is a favourite Maugham theme; European notions of honour are sometimes disastrous at home, but they need to be practised with even more astuteness in the Pacific. Instead, Lawson treats Ethel as a European, and is bewildered when she does not make what he considers is the appropriate response. Their cultural differences are brought sharply into focus on the occasion when he beats her. Samoan women accept a beating as part of their lot. Though Ethel's and Lawson's relationship has deteriorated considerably by the time he beats her, his display of aggression comes close to reawakening her love.

> He threw the whip away from him and rushed out of the room. Ethel heard him go and stopped crying. She looked around cautiously, then raised herself. She was sore, but she had not been badly hurt, and she looked at her dress to see if it was damaged. The native women are not unused to blows. What he had done did not outrage her. When she looked at herself in the glass and arranged her hair, her eyes were shining. There was a strange look in them. Perhaps then she was nearer loving him than she had ever been before. (I.144)

As far as Ethel is concerned, Lawson has done no more than many men in her society do. But Lawson feels that he has broken one of the sacred laws of society—that a man should not beat his wife. His abject apology at once arouses her scorn and costs him his advantage. Maugham skilfully suggests that while Europeans will tolerate a woman beating her husband—many are amused at the way Chaplin's Australian wife uses her fists and feet to keep him in order—they will not tolerate a man beating his wife. Miller's intervention brings the whole sordid relationship between Ethel and Lawson to a tragic climax.

Their tragedy however, results from more than a straightforward conflict of social and cultural *mores*. Ethel is a half-caste. Even in her native Samoa she occupies an ambiguous position. (I. 131,132) Furthermore, as the narrator is at pains to point out, she is not a typical half-caste. She has, for example, none of the 'exuberance common to the half-caste'. (I. 147) She is unusually beautiful.

> Her features were lovely; but I think what struck me most was the delicacy of her appearance; the half-castes as a rule have a certain coarseness, they seem a little roughly formed, but she had an exquisite daintiness that took your breath away. (I. 123)

Unlike the other natives and half-castes 'who bathe in bands, laughing and joyous, the whole family together', Ethel bathes alone. (I. 126)

By emphasising her individuality Maugham makes her more than a beautiful half-caste; she becomes Lawson's *femme fatale*. Part of the conflict between them arises from his attempts to penetrate her mystery. He is not only infatuated with her beauty, but wants to possess her in the hope that he will be able to understand her. (I. 133,136). Maugham uses the symbol of the pool to represent Ethel's mysteriousness.

> There was a little river that bubbled over the rocks in a swift stream, and then, after forming the deep pool, ran on, shallow and crystalline ... it had a tropical richness, a passion, a scented languor which seemed to melt the heart. The water was fresh, but not cold; and it was delicious after the heat of the day. To bathe there refreshed not only the body but the soul. (I. 123,124)

Like the pool, Ethel is exotic and sensual. She can be both dark and deep, and, as the narrator suspects, shallow and superficial. The topography of the pool echoes the shape of her personality.

> In her pretty pink frock and high-heeled shoes she looked quite European. You could hardly have guessed at that dark background of native life in which she felt herself so much more at home. I did not imagine that she was at all intelligent, and I should not have been surprised if a man, after living with her for some time, had found the passion which had drawn him to her sink into boredom. (I. 148).

Ethel is attracted to the pool as an image of herself. It is understandable then that when she finally rejects Lawson she drives him from the pool (l. 147); and that his last desperate act is to drown himself in it.

Maugham is more interested in the human aspects of the story than in creating a story with suspense. Very early, in a number of terse statements made by Chaplin, we are told most of what will happen. (l. 119). The history of Ethel's and Lawson's relationship is then recounted through a flashback (l. 123, 147), which gives the reader a sense of *déjà vu*. Our attention is directed to what has happened rather than to what will happen. That the narrator is primarily interested in the human aspect of his story is clearly indicated in two passages; a rhetorical question:

> Who would have thought that this wretched object was in his way a romantic figure or that his life had in it those elements of pity and terror which the theorist tells us are necessary to achieve the effect of tragedy? (l. 120).

and a statement:

> I held my breath, for to me there is nothing more awe-inspiring than when a man discovers to you the nakedness of his soul. Then you see that no one is so trivial or debased but that in him is a spark of something to excite compassion. (l. 151).

Above all, the narrator of 'The Pool' asks his audience to ponder the tragic decline of a man.

NOTES AND GLOSSARY:
(*a*) In 'Rain' Maugham wrote about two white people in the tropics. In 'The Pool' he writes about a white man and a native woman.
(*b*) The transition from first person narrator ('I . . .') to omniscient author ('He . . .') is skilfully done (l. 123, 'He had but . . .'); as is the reverse operation. (l. 147, 'I met Ethel . . .')
(*c*) The first person narrator continues on p.147 the first impressions that he had formed of Ethel, recorded on p.123.
(*d*) The narrator's attitude changes as he becomes acquainted with Lawson's history. This is skilful. He gradually wins our sympathy as he unfolds the story, a movement that parallels our own reception of the story. At first we are sceptical, but as the evidence mounts up, we accept more and more.
(*e*) Perhaps the weakest point in the story is the failure to explain how Ethel secures the money to buy her ticket to Samoa without her husband's knowledge. He is a bank employee.
(*f*) That Lawson remains unaware of the social consequences of his marriage until the birth of his first child is realistic, and enhances the credibility of the story. His reasons for his drinking are also credible.

tipsy: slightly drunk
He was a character: He was a memorable person, a vivid personality
a 'good sport': a good fellow
beanos: drinking sprees
'wet' nights: drinking sprees
Missus: wife
couldn't stand it: was beyond endurance
cubby hole: very small room
fairly soused: very drunk
climb on the waggon and stay there: remain sober
I was all over the place: I liked the place very much
Robert Louis Stevenson: (1850–94). Scottish novelist and essayist, author of *Treasure Island, Dr Jekyll and Mr Hyde,* and *Kidnapped.* Towards the end of his life he settled in Samoa where he wrote *The Beach of Falesá* (1892), *A Footnote to History* (1892), and *In the South Seas* (1896)
dressed up to the nines: dressed in their best clothes
By George!: exclamation of surprise. Short for 'By Saint George'
'And when so sad . . . : The lines, which are misquoted, are from 'In No Strange Land', by Francis Thompson (1859–1907), an English poet who was an opium addict: 'But (when so sad thou canst not sadder)/ Cry;—and upon thy so sore loss/ Shall shine the traffic of Jacob's ladder/ Pitched betwixt Heaven and Charing Cross'
'The Hound of Heaven': Thompson's most famous poem. A rich and passionate musing on the conflict between sacred and profane love. Published in *Poems* (1893)
It's a bit of all right: It is very good
My lungs are a bit dicky: My lungs are weak
time for a drain: time for a drink
all and sundry: everbody
his head reeled: he felt overcome by a powerful feeling
Talofa: Greetings (Samoan)
at one time fairly well to do: at one time moderately wealthy
She's a peach: she is very good looking
I've given her the glad eye once or twice, but I guess there's nothing doing: I have hinted at a sexual relationship once or twice, but she has not responded
rude chaff: coarse jokes
wound received in a scrap: wound received in a fight
lounging about: indolently inactive
Ethel's just titivating: Ethel is just smartening up her appearance

higgledy-piggledy:	disordered
rid of the hotel:	not having to live at the hotel
'He doesn't know what he is up against', said Nelson. 'Someone ought to put him wise.':	'He is unaware of the trouble he will have to face', said Nelson. 'Someone ought to advise him.'
This child ain't taking any, I'll tell the world:	I am not going to do what he has done
look upon him as a gold mine:	look upon him as someone with a lot of money
They're as dull as ditchwater:	They are boring
a rum place:	an unlikely or unusual place
bolted:	left suddenly and without warning
like a house of cards:	like something very insubstantial
was given a nip:	was given a drink
a shack:	a small house
blind drunk:	very drunk
gave him the cold shoulder:	deliberately ignored him
why he should put on airs:	why he should pretend to be important
made a bad bargain:	made a poor choice
monkey tricks:	deception
something up his sleeve:	a secret advantage over
carrying on:	having a secret love affair
to fork out money:	to pay for
held the purse-strings:	controlled the finances
before you can say knife:	within an instant
put up with any hanky-panky:	tolerate any immoral behaviour
to gad about by yourself:	(in this context) to visit by yourself
hangers-on:	uninvited associates, companions
cheek by jowl:	in close proximity
a pretty ugly customer:	a very unpleasant person who may become violent
put a bullet into:	shoot
Hang it all:	exclamation of despair and frustration
common flower of the hedgerow:	common native flower
Gets my dander up:	makes me angry
If he hadn't, he'd have had the whip hand over her:	if he had not, he would have been in command of the situation
yaller:	yellow, that is cowardly, cowardice
as happy as lords:	very happy
dead struck on:	very much in love with
make a dash for it:	suddenly leave
me for my mosquito net:	I am going to bed
a dip:	a swim

'**Black as the pit from pole to pole:** from 'Invictus', a poem by William Ernest Henley (1849–1903), an English poet: 'Out of the night that covers me,/ Black as the pit from pole to pole,/ I thank whatever gods may be/ For my unconquerable soul.
In the fell clutch of circumstance/ I have not winced nor cried aloud./ Under the bludgeonings of chance/ My head is bloody, but unbow'd.
Beyond this place of wrath and tears/ Looms but the Horror of the shade,/ And yet the menace of the years/ Finds and shall find me unafraid.'

Appearance and reality

SETTING: Paris.

CHARACTERS: Mademoiselle Lisette Larion, a mannequin. Madame Saladin, her aunt. Monsieur Raymond Le Sueur, a member of the Senate.

PUBLICATION: In the *International Magazine*, November 1934; *Nash's Magazine*, December 1934; and *Creatures of Circumstance* (1947).

SUMMARY OF THE PLOT: A distinguished French Senator, Monsieur Le Sueur, is taken to a private showing of the spring collection of a leading fashion house by his wife. He is attracted to one of the mannequins, Lisette Larion. From closely observing her reaction to his polite greeting he deduces that she is respectable, discreet, and unattached. He hires a detective to check her background, and obtain the address of the aunt with whom she boards. His secretary calls on the aunt and invites her and her niece to dine with the Senator at one of the most expensive restaurants in Paris. Lisette becomes his mistress. He leases an apartment for her, and has it tastefully furnished.

All goes well for the next two years until the Senator, returning unexpectedly from his constituency one weekend, discovers that Lisette has herself taken a lover—a young commercial traveller. He orders the young man out of the apartment, and upbraids Lisette for her ingratitude. She bears his accusations and reproaches with disarming self-possession. She suggests that in taking a lover for herself she has done no more than he has in taking her as his mistress. Monsieur Le Sueur realises that he has met his match. But his vanity is wounded. One way of regaining his honour, Lisette insinuates, is to settle a substantial dowry on her. This will induce the young man to marry her. As he is a commercial traveller, he will only be at home at the weekends. Instead of suffering like an outraged husband, Monsieur Le Sueur can take matters into his own hands, reverse the tables, and resume his role as her lover. The practicality of her scheme appeals to his common sense, its frankness to his sense of realism, and its panache to his sense of dignity and humour. Lisette marries her young commercial traveller in a ceremony witnessed by Monsieur Le Sueur and her aunt. The wedding service is a tissue of clichés about the sanctity of marriage to which the Senator responds with befitting dignity, and a demure Lisette with becoming modesty. The situation has been saved. Both appearance and reality have been preserved. At the end, the Senator reflects that he has undoubtedly improved his situation. He is about to become a Minister in the Government, and so it is better that his mistress should be a respectable married woman rather than a little mannequin.

ANALYSIS: 'Appearance and Reality' is a deftly constructed comedy. After careful consideration a leading politician takes a nineteen-year-old mannequin for a mistress. Almost two years of genuine happiness pass, and then he discovers her in bed with a young man. The result could easily be tragic, but it is not. The young woman skilfully persuades the politician to give her a dowry so she can marry the young man. This makes her happy. The young man's profession takes him away for most of the week so the politician can still come and visit her. This makes him happy.

The events leading up to this eminently rational settlement in which everyone's desires are satisfied, are illuminated by moments of genuine comedy. The young man, for example, cannot leave the bed where he has been surprised with Lisette because the Senator is standing between him and his clothes.

> 'What are you waiting for?' shouted the Senator. 'Do you want me to use force?'
> 'He can't go out in his pyjamas', said Lisette.
> 'They're not his pyjamas, they're my pyjamas.'
> 'He's waiting for his clothes.'
> Monsieur Le Sueur looked round and on the chair behind him, flung down in a disorderly fashion, was a variety of masculine garments. The Senator gave the young man a look of contempt.
> 'You may take your clothes, Monsieur,' he said with cold disdain. (I.196)

Such strongly realised and genuinely humorous scenes mitigate the possibility of tragedy.

The final settlement is arrived at without either Lisette or Monsieur Le Sueur sacrificing any of their appeal. Maugham never allows us, for example, to feel repulsed by Lisette's cool, calculated approach. We so admire the way she keeps her head that we never think of her as scheming. Her full response to her aunt's relaying of Monsieur Le Sueur's invitation to dinner consists of just the right mixture of hauteur, individuality, and opportunism. Her initial *'cette vieille carpe'* and her *'Et ta soeur'* are sufficiently irreverent to establish her independence; the astute question about where they are to dine and her reaction to the reply assure us of her *savoir-faire*. The fact that she is not corrupted by the money that Monsieur Le Sueur lavishes on her further endears her to us. If anything, her thrift, her prudence, and her accomplishments as a cook, a housekeeper, a companion, a conversationalist, and a lover, come dangerously close to rendering her too perfect to be credible. It is therefore reassuring to discover that she has retained her independence, though the situation in which Monsieur Le Sueur discovers her with the young silk traveller is extremely awkward. She wins our admiration by the way she extricates herself. She is courageous; she does not turn and run. She is diplomatic; she lets him talk himself out of anger into self-pity and then orders breakfast for him when she discovers he is hungry. She is a psychologist; she uses a leaven of flattery to re-establish his self-confidence:

'It is obvious your friend has no education.'
'Of course he has not your distinction', murmured Lisette.
'And has he my intelligence?'
'Oh, no.'
'Is he rich?'
'Penniless.'
'Then, name of a name, what is it you see in him?'   (I.197)

Her reply, though frank, is not unkind.

'He's young,' smiled Lisette.
The Senator looked down at his plate and a tear rose in his eyes and rolled down his cheek into his coffee. Lisette gave him a kindly look.
'My poor friend, one cannot have everything in this life,' she said. (I.198)

Her explanation of her twin allegiance is so disarmingly honest that it transcends self-justification.

'I love you because you are so distinguished and your conversation is instructive and interesting. I love you because you are kind and generous. I love him because his eyes are so big and his hair waves and he dances divinely. It's very natural.'   (I.198)

Lisette also has the *savoir-faire* merely to hint at the possible solution. By allowing Monsieur Le Sueur to assume the initiative she makes him feel that he has always been in control. Her final obedience to his request that she give up work when she gets married is not so much a defeat as a strategic withdrawal. She has achieved what she wants; why strive for something which may cost her all she has won?

Lisette's skill however, is not allowed to overshadow that displayed by Monsieur Le Sueur. Maugham gives the story a pleasing symmetry by according him the final victory; it is better for him to have a mistress who is a respectable married woman than to have a mere slip of a mannequin. Monsieur Le Sueur's revelation of this fact gives the story an unexpected twist. We perhaps suspect, when Lisette's affair is discovered, that with Monsieur Le Sueur's and her temperament the situation will be resolved, but we are surprised to discover that the result is to their mutual advantage. The advantage for Lisette is so obvious that we tend to forget Monsieur Le Sueur.

Finally, Maugham's skilful use of a first person narrator greatly enhances the artistic success of the story. The narrator's opening remark, 'I do not vouch for the truth of this story ...', is effective. It divests him of the responsibility of making all the details of his story plausible, and it encourages us as readers to surrender more of ourselves than usual to him. We generally allow far more to someone who claims he may be telling the truth than to someone who asserts that he is. At first the way in which Maugham's narrator appears to enumerate the qualities of *'gauloiserie'*, *'bons sens'*, and *'panache'*, and his cavalier familiarity with *Appearance and Reality* ('even though the lay reader') threaten to alienate him from us as an ostentatiously hearty pedant. It is not until he reduces his rather lengthy description of Lisette's occupation to 'She was in short a mannequin' that we detect the irony that is constantly undercutting this pretentiousness.

The narrator's irony is brilliantly focused in at least three places in the story. The first is his description of Monsieur Le Sueur's family.

> The marriage had been a success. She had provided him with a son who could play tennis nearly as well as a professional, dance quite as well as a gigolo, and hold his own at bridge with any of the experts; and a daughter whom he had been able to dower sufficiently to marry to a very nearly authentic prince. He had reason to be proud of his children. (I. 190)

The repetition of 'nearly' and the last sentence are definitely tongue in cheek. Such accomplishments are, of course, singularly unimpressive. The second use of irony is the lengthy interjection following Lisette's *'Et ta soeur.'*

> This phrase, which of course means: and your sister, sounds harmless enough, and even pointless, is a trifle vulgar and is used by well-brought-up young women, I think, only if they want to shock. It expresses the most forcible unbelief, and the only correct translation into the vernacular is too coarse for my chaste pen. (I. 193)

This elaborate apology makes us party to a code of ethics where discreet adultery is countenanced, but open profanity is abhorred. Morality is preserved only in the niceties of speech. The third occasion is similar.

> He stroked his handsome square beard with a composed and dignified gesture.
> 'Not a row of beans,' he replied, but the expression had a Gallic breadth that would perhaps have given his more conservative supporters something of a shock.   (I. 200)

In Monsieur Le Sueur's gesture, and in the explanation of his expression, are encapsulated the theme of appearance and reality. The story satisfies us as a comedy because reason restrains emotion, and the sordid is always translated into something so clever that it arouses our admiration.

NOTES AND GLOSSARY:
(a) Maugham reinforces the French setting by using expressions such as '*tiens*,' '*petit déjeuner*,' '*dot*,' and '*bonsoir*'. They are used sparingly, as are the obvious transliterations of French expressions. For example: 'It's love, by blue,' he muttered. By blue is an adaptation of the French *parbleu* (for *pardieu*, by God!)
(b) The story points to an interesting comparison between the English and the French. The Englishman writes a book on Appearance and Reality. The Frenchman conducts his love affair with due regard to both.

horse sense: common sense
Appearance and Reality: by F.H. Bradley. A reference to *Appearance and Reality: A Metaphysical Essay* (1893)
nothing matters a hang anyway: nothing is of any importance
by blue: an adaptation of *parbleu*, by God!
bureau de tabac: (*French*) tobacconist
concierge: a caretaker of a block of flats
a slap-up dinner: an excellent dinner
Tête à tête: (*French*) in intimate conversation
Tiens!: (*French*) exclamation of surprise—Heavens!
in the blackest colours: emphasising the worst
petit déjeuner: (*French*) breakfast, the morning meal
O tempora, o mores: (*Latin*) A quotation from Cicero: Oh, the times! Oh, the manners! A complaint about the evilness of the day
Not a row of beans: Not at all
a dot of a million francs: a dowry of a million francs
a horse of another colour: a different matter, or case
Romeo and Juliet: two lovers immortalised by the English dramatist Shakespeare in a play of that name

Paul and Virginia: the principal characters in an ideal love story by the French writer, Bernard de Saint Pierre (1737-1814), in a novel of that name published in 1787
Daphnis and Chloe: famous lovers in Greek mythology

The Voice of the Turtle

SETTING: A small flat in London. The narrator's villa and La Falterona's villa on the Riviera.

CHARACTERS: Peter Melrose, a young English novelist. La Falterona, a celebrated prima donna. Miss Glaser, her English secretary.

PUBLICATION: *Nash's Magazine*, January 1935; the *International Magazine*, November 1936; and *The Mixture as Before* (1940).

SUMMARY OF THE PLOT: An un-named author, who narrates the story, is invited to a small sherry party in Bloomsbury to meet Peter Melrose, a young English writer who has caused a sensation with his first novel. The narrator finds him raw, disputatious, and crude, but he is moved by his obvious sincerity and his vitality. He leaves the party never expecting to see him again.

Two or three days later he receives an autographed copy of the novel in the mail. Its coarseness offends him, but he is impressed by Peter Melrose's lucid style, by the sure touch of some of the descriptive passages, and by the intense passion that burns in the lives of the major characters. He sends Peter a critique of his novel, and invites him to lunch. Over lunch he discovers that he is looking for somewhere quiet to write his next novel, so he invites him to his villa on the Riviera.

The narrator returns to the South of France, and a month later is joined by Peter, who tells him about his book. It will be a romantic story about a young writer and a celebrated prima donna. The writer will be an inveterate dreamer, obscure, and rather unattractive; the prima donna will be young, beautiful, fiery, wilful, highly intelligent, and magnanimous. The narrator thinks his conception of the heroine rather naive, so he arranges for Peter to meet a prima donna who is famous for her voice and her lovers, La Falterona.

La Falterona's dining with them is a resounding success. She talks endlessly about herself; her life, the intrigues of her numerous lovers, and the machinations of the impresarios, managers, critics, and other singers, who seem to have attacked her at all points in her career. The narrator feels sure that these disclosures have shown her to be vindictive, selfish, scheming, mercenary, and incredibly vain. He is certain that Peter Melrose will have to revise radically his conception of his heroine. To his amazement Peter enthuses about the parallels between La

Falterona and his prima donna. The narrator maintains a discreet silence. Several days later Peter leaves. The novel, when it is published, is given a guarded reception. The narrator finds it uneven; the humour is unnecessarily coarse, but the period setting is skilfully reconstructed, and the love affair between the young writer and the prima donna throbs with genuine passion.

A year passes. La Falterona tours South America. On her return she invites the narrator to dinner. She attacks him for setting her up to be used as copy by a second-rate novelist; she has read Peter Melrose's book. The narrator points out that there are a number of discrepancies between the heroine's and her personalities. She retorts that her friends have called it a *roman à clef*, and she points to an incident that she had told Peter, and that he had written into his book. The incident, and her subsequent treatment of her secretary, confirms the narrator in his opinion of her. La Falterona ignores his censures. She goes to the window and sings, first some light airs from Schumann, and then Isolde's death song from Wagner's *Tristan and Isolde*. Her singing is profoundly moving. Her voice is powerful, yet controlled; her intonation is perfect; her interpretation and shading are exquisite. The narrator realises that he prefers her as she is, unpleasant but supremely gifted. She is more forceful in the flesh than she could ever be in a novel.

ANALYSIS: 'The Voice of The Turtle' demonstrates Maugham's skill at constructing an excellent short story from what on analysis seems unpromising material. The sherry party at which the narrator meets the young novelist, the dinner with the flamboyant prima donna, the reception of Peter Melrose's second novel, and the subsequent evening at La Falterona's are all rather slight in themselves. But fused together and given the tone of the narrator's distinctive point of view, the individual elements become an integral part of an impressive whole. When we reach the end of the story and share the emotions aroused by La Falterona's rendition of Isolde's death song, we can look back and see how each event has been skilfully used to prepare us for the concluding experience. The sherry party shows us that the narrator, though detached, cynical, and worldly, is fascinated by passion and attracted to vitality. The critique of Peter Melrose's first novel, the invitation to lunch, and the suggestion to the young novelist that he may like to join him for a few days at his villa on the Riviera, establish the narrator as someone who is fundamentally generous. His silence at Peter's obvious naivety after they have dined with La Falterona reveals tolerance and discretion. His response to the second novel shows he is a man of experience and taste. The manner in which he handles La Falterona's accusation that he has merely used her for copy marks him as a person who can judge the limits of frankness. The cumulative effect of these revelations is to establish the narrator in our minds as someone who possesses impeccable taste, and whose response to art is unquestionably genuine. When we read at the end of the story that his heart 'melted' within him when he heard La Falterona sing, and that he had a 'most awkward lump' in his throat when she finished, we willingly allow him these emotions. We do not accuse him of exaggeration; nor do we think that he is being sentimental. That we should respect his response and to some extent share his emotion is important. The narrator's experience provides the climax of the story. The last few paragraphs of 'The Voice of the Turtle' evoke a mood, and if this mood is to be at once shared and credible then our faith in the man who is recounting the experience must have been firmly established. The story succeeds because we have been prepared for the narrator's final experience.

That 'The Voice of the Turtle' ends with an account of an experience rather than a dénouement makes it unusual among Maugham's short stories. He generally preferred to write the type of story that had a definite plot, a specific number of sharply delineated characters, and possessed what he was fond of calling 'a beginning, a middle, and an end.' The beginning of a short story he believed should establish the setting with brevity and clarity, introduce the main characters, and initiate the action; the middle should mark the zenith of the action; and the end should be a satisfactory conclusion that unquestionably accounted for all the elements of the plot. A definite plot, he argued, provided a clear line of direction for the reader and a distinct set of limits for the writer. It enabled him to distinguish with ease what was relevant and what was irrelevant. The success of this type of story depends largely on the plot. A strong plot can make a good story. The plot always matters as much as, sometimes more than, the characters.

The success of a story like 'The Voice of the Turtle', where there is very little plot, depends largely on the characters. If they are strongly realised, consistent, and credible, then the reader will be able to project himself unreservedly into the emotional centre of the story. Since there is very little plot, the characters must give the story shape. The great danger with stories like 'The Voice of the Turtle' is that they will sprawl, or tail off inconclusively.

'The Voice of the Turtle' is a good story because the characters are excellent. Peter Melrose is an engaging mixture of the hard-boiled youth and the sensitive young man. La Falterona is larger than life without being gargantuan. Unquestionably the most successful 'character' however is the narrator, the 'I' who tells the story. At first he seems unnecessarily cynical in his dismissal of sections of the literary establishment: 'Elderly gentleman with nothing much to do but go to luncheon parties praised [the novel] with girlish enthusiasm, and wiry little women who didn't get on with their husbands thought it showed promise.' (I. 268) But he redeems himself when he defends Peter Melrose's right to be breezy, outspoken, and assertive.

> It is very natural that clever young men should be rather odious. They are conscious of gifts that they do not know how to use. They are exasperated with the world that will not recognise their merit. They have something to give, and no hand is stretched out to receive it. They are impatient for the fame they regard as their due. No, I do not mind odious young men; it is when they are charming that I button up the pockets of my sympathy. (I. 271)

This is both witty and engaging. For the remainder of the story we surrender ourselves to the narrator, confident that though he does not suffer fools gladly, he is not devoid of generosity or a sense of humour.

The least satisfactory parts of 'The Voice of the Turtle' are the two incidents from La Falterona's love life, the story of the emerald ring, and the story of the string of pearls. Though they add to our understanding of her character, they are not fully integrated into the body of the story. They interrupt the flow of the narrative. Furthermore the narrator's method of introducing the first incident: 'The story of the emerald ring was this: ....' (I. 281) is surprisingly artless.

These are minor flaws however in what is otherwise an excellent story. Without the assistance of a strong plot, Maugham has written a poignant and compelling account of how an urbane, worldly-wise writer, whose feelings are not easily reached, yields to his emotions at the sound of a beautiful song.

NOTES AND GLOSSARY:
(a) Maugham was told the story of the emerald ring by Lily Langtry. See *A Writer's Notebook*, pp.94–5.

(b) La Falterona changes her accent or the intonation of her voice several times in the story.
> She claimed to be a Hungarian, but her English was perfect; she spoke it with a slight accent (when she remembered), but with an intonation suggestive, I have been told, of Kansas City. (I. 274).... for her accent at the beginning of the dinner was quite Sevillian. (I. 275).... with a strong South American accent. (I. 279)

This brilliantly emphasises her falseness and her delight in playing roles.

(c) 'I think you must make sure not to divide the interest in a story.' *A Writer's Notebook*, p. 295. Maugham avoids this pitfall in 'The Voice of the Turtle' by skilfully transferring our attention from Peter Melrose to La Falterona through the single theme of fiction versus life.

I could not make up my mind: I could not reach a decision
caused some stir: caused a sensation
always on the lookout: always watching for
like a good tramp in the rain: like a long walk in the rain
never done a stroke of work: never done any work
Boofuls: Beautiful; a pet name
King's Road, Chelsea: a fashionable street in London
no sooner was my back turned than they would tear my own to shreds:
    No sooner had I left the room than they would begin to criticise me
tailed off: was inconclusive
That was passion all right: That was certainly passion
we made a date: we made an appointment
bored stiff: very bored
I sent him a wire: I sent him a telegram
Ouida: pen name for Marie Louise de la Ramée (1839–1908), a popular English romantic novelist and journalist
This hard-boiled youth to write: This cynical and experienced youth to write
and I was tickled: and I was amused
Edwardian: A period of English history marked by the reign of Edward VII, 1901 to 1910
I've hunted around in all sorts of byways: I have looked in a large number of unusual places
Melba: Dame Nellie Melba (1862–1931), a famous Australian soprano whose real name was Nellie Porter Mitchell
who were never able to put it over the public: who were never able to deceive the public
should get his money's worth: should have the best opportunity
a line of glib chatter: a collection of superficial sayings
bunkum: an expression of disgust at insincere talk
He ate her words: He paid close attention to what she said
how she had the nerve: how she was able to
twopenny-halfpenny: obscure, second-rate, amateur
Come off it: exclamation of disbelief
was roughed out: had written out a general plan
Florence Montgomerie: Fictional character (?) invented by Maugham. Richard Barkley, *The Road to Mayerling*, London, 1959, indicates in several places that there were many rumours that Prince Rudolf carried on miscellaneous amours, but claims that most of these were unfounded

Crown Prince Rudolf: Crown Prince Rudolf (1858–89). Austrian Archduke and Crown Prince. The only son of the Emperor Franz Joseph and the Empress Elizabeth. Entered into a suicide pact with Baroness Mary Vesta, a young girl of seventeen, in 1889

Lola Montez: stage name of Marie Dolores Eliza Rosanna Gilbert (1818?–61), a dancer and adventuress, born in Limerick, Ireland. Mistress of Louis I of Bavaria 1847–8

Nell Gwyn and Charles II: Nell Gwyn (1650–87), English actress, mistress of Charles II (1630–85). Originally an orange-seller at Drury Lane Theatre, she became Charles's mistress some time in the 1660s

are as mean as cat's meat: are very mean

I was mad: I was angry

I had him eating out of my hand: I caused him to become very attentive and polite

all that food you walloped down: all that food you ate

'Mild und leise wie er lächelt Wie das Auge er öffnet': Wagner, *Tristan and Isolde*, Act III, ii. A misquotation. It should read: *Mild und leise wie er lächelt, wie das Auge hold er öffnet.* Mild and softly he is smiling: how his eyelids sweetly open!

The Unconquered

SETTING: A French farm, ten to fifteen kilometres from Soissons.

CHARACTERS: Hans and Willi, two German soldiers. Monsieur and Madame Périer, a French farmer and his wife. Their only daughter, Annette. Pierre Gavin, her fiancé, a prisoner-of-war in a German camp.

PUBLICATION: Originally published on its own as a limited edition in 1944, and then included in *Creatures of Circumstance* (1947).

SUMMARY OF THE PLOT: 'The Unconquered' is set in occupied France at the height of the Second World War. Two German soldiers, Hans and Willi, who have lost their way, call at a farmhouse to ask directions for Soissons. The door is answered by the farmer's only daughter, Annette, who feigns ignorance of the locality. They push past her and go into the kitchen where the farmer, Monsieur Périer, and his wife are finishing their evening meal. As Hans is thirsty he buys two bottles of wine, opens one, and sits down to have a friendly chat. The Périers respond to his cordiality with stony silence. He turns to Annette and demands a kiss. She refuses, and there is a struggle. Monsieur Périer is knocked unconscious, his wife is pushed against the wall, and Annette is dragged into the next room by Hans, where she is raped. She falls into a dead faint. Hans and Willi finish their wine and leave the farmhouse.

Three months pass. After the fall of Paris Hans is posted back to Soissons. One day, out of idle curiosity and a desire to make amends for what he had done, he revisits the farm. He takes a pair of silk stockings with him as a present. Annette is at home by herself. She scornfully rejects his apology and his present, and treats him with undisguised contempt. He is not disconcerted. In her anger and her scorn Annette appears more attractive than he had at first noticed. He realises that she is sensitive, cultured, very intelligent, and refined. It seems that her family have very little to eat, so when he begins to visit the farm regularly he always brings a small food parcel with him. His bluff good nature and his desire to please gradually win over Monsieur Périer and his wife, but Annette remains fiercely hostile. One day he discovers that she is pregnant with his child. He is overcome by powerful feelings, and realises that he has fallen deeply in love with her. A few days later he goes to the farm to propose to her. Either she can come to Germany with him or he can stay in France and go into partnership with her father. The Périers, who have lost their son, consider this an attractive proposition, but Annette angrily refuses. She has a fiancé, a fellow schoolteacher, Pierre Gavin, who is a prisoner-of-war in a German camp. She wants to marry only him. But Hans persists, and his hopes rise when on one of his visits to the farm he discovers that Pierre has been shot for inciting a riot. He presses his love for her, but her revulsion for him has been transformed into hatred by Pierre's death. Her only thought is revenge. How can she wound him as deeply as he has wounded her? She realises that his joyous anticipation of a son will provide her with the means. The time for her confinement arrives, and she is delivered of a fine, healthy boy who is the image of his father. The next day Hans comes to the farm, and when he learns of the birth he demands to see his son. Madame Périer goes to fetch him, but Annette and the baby have disappeared. There is a moment of panic, then the back door opens and Annette staggers in. She is wet and cold. She has drowned Hans's baby in the nearby brook.

ANALYSIS: 'The Unconquered' is the only story Maugham wrote that is set in the Second World War. It is a stark portrayal of different kinds of evil; the evil that follows an impulsive act, and the evil of a premeditated crime.

When Hans first comes to the farmhouse he does not intend to rape Annette. In several places in the story, (I. 308, 309, 311, 315), it is made clear that his impulsive act is the result of a number of circumstances. He is very tired after his long ride on his motorcycle, yet strangely elated by the ease with which his countrymen have defeated the English and the French. The bottle of wine that he drinks on an empty stomach makes him slightly drunk. He becomes irritated by the Périers' sullen silence, and he feels like humiliating Annette for her haughtiness. The struggle and her blows excite him. She is easily conquered by his physical strength. All these extenuating circumstances make the story more credible, and they heighten the clash between his impulsive act and her carefully planned revenge.

As time passes the event becomes less and less significant in Hans's mind. When he first returns to the farm he smiles disarmingly at Annette and says: 'Why do you look so cross? I didn't do you much harm you know.' (I. 312) On his next visit he tries to play down even further what he has done. 'After all, it was an accident, that time I came here with Willi. You needn't be afraid of me. I'll respect Annette as if she was my own sister.' (I. 315) These attempts to rob the event of its significance, and the clumsy but obviously sincere way he tries to make amends, influence Annette's parents. When Madame Périer tells him that Annette is pregnant, she seems completely resigned to what has happened. 'She began to talk, not bitterly, not blaming him even, but as though it were a misfortune of nature, like a cow dying in giving birth to a calf or a sharp spring frost nipping the fruit trees and ruining the crop, a misfortune that human kind must accept with resignation and humility.' (I. 319) Monsieur Périer adopts a similar attitude. 'I went through the last war and we all did things we wouldn't have done in peacetime. Human nature is human nature.' (I. 323) The more they get to know Hans, and the more they come to see him as their future son-in-law, the more they try to lessen the significance of his raping Annette. 'What have you got against the boy?', Madame Périer exclaims in the face of her daughter's implacable hatred.

> 'He took you by force—yes, he was drunk at the time. It's not the first time that's happened to a woman and it won't be the last time. He hit your father and he bled like a pig, but does your father bear him malice?'
>
> 'It was an unpleasant incident, but I've forgotten it,' said Périer. (I. 328)

Their overwhelming desire to replace their dead son and to secure their farm leads them to blur the distinction between a blow in the face and being raped.

But Annette, as the one who has suffered, refuses to excuse or explain away what Hans has done. She is persistently uncooperative. She refuses to give Hans and Willi directions when they first come to the farmhouse.

She angrily refuses the food he brings, and pours scorn on his attempts to ingratiate himself with her and her parents. She hates him with a fierce hatred from the first time she sees him until the day that she drowns his child. Only once, when he comes to see her after he has received the news that Pierre has been killed and tells her how much he is looking forward to the birth of his son, does she waver.

> He sighed and rose to his feet. When he closed the door behind him she watched him walk down the pathway that led to the road. She realised with rage that some of the things he said had aroused in her heart a feeling that she had never felt for him before. 'O God, give me strength,' she cried.   (I. 331)

But when she sees him kick the old farm dog that he has tried for so long to befriend, she renews her determination to make him suffer as much as she can. Maugham brilliantly makes this trivial incident the occasion for her terrible resolve. It is often the little things, as he so rightly implies, that tip the balance.

Through Annette, Maugham shows how a person can become so obsessed by revenge that they lose their humanity. She commits infanticide to avenge her rape and the killing of Pierre by drowning the child Hans has fathered. In order to commit this terrible murder she has forcibly to suppress one of the strongest human instincts, the desire of a mother to love and protect her newborn child. For nine months she thinks only of hatred and revenge, and this gives her the strength to carry out her plan. Her only fear is that her natural instincts will prove too strong. 'I had to do it at once', she cries as she staggers into the house at the end of the story. 'I was afraid if I waited I shouldn't have the courage'. (I. 334) Her fierce hatred enables her to convert murder into revenge.

Annette's realisation of the most effective way of revenging herself on Hans is the weakest aspect of the story. Up to this point Maugham has carefully avoided the theatrical. The various confrontations between different characters and the emotions they display have been rendered in short, sharp scenes of tightly controlled prose. There is, for example, the opening paragraph:

> He came back into the kitchen. The man was still on the floor, lying where he had hit him, and his face was bloody. He was moaning. The woman had backed against the wall and was staring with terrified eyes at Willi, his friend, and when he came in she gave a gasp and broke into loud sobbing. Willi was sitting at the table, his revolver in his hand, with a half empty glass of wine beside him. Hans went up to the table, filled his glass and emptied it at a gulp.   (I. 307)

The short, bare phrases and sentences are very effective. But Annette's resolve to commit some terrible act of revenge is repeated a number of times:

> She looked at him intently and there was a strange gleam in her eyes. You would have said it was a look of triumph. She gave a short laugh. (I. 330)
> She stared at him with hard, hard eyes. Her face was set and stern. An idea, a terrible idea, was forming itself in her mind. (I. 331)
> There was a looking-glass hanging by the side of the door and she looked at herself in it. She drew herself up and smiled at her reflection. But rather than a smile it was a fiendish grimace. (I. 332)

By over-emphasising the moment Annette realises that murdering the child will secure her revenge, Maugham detracts from the force of the ending. The 'strange gleam', the 'terrible idea', and the 'fiendish grimace' are too theatrical. They push the story from tragedy towards melodrama.

'The Unconquered' can be read on more than one level. At the literal level it is the story of a wronged girl's terrible revenge. At the symbolic level Annette represents the spirit of France. She embodies the essential difference between conquest and defeat. 'I live only to see the deliverance of France,' she tells Hans.

> It'll come, perhaps not next year or the year after, perhaps not for thirty years, but it'll come. The rest of them can do what they like, I will never come to terms with the invaders of my country. I hate you and I hate this child that you have given me. Yes, we've been defeated. Before the end comes you'll see that we haven't been conquered. (I. 331)

One country may occupy another, but it can never crush it by any other means than genocide. Human beings will go to any lengths to assert their independence and freedom. Though Annette remains unconquered the price of her victory is high. It costs her her humanity.

NOTES AND GLOSSARY:

(a) The symmetry of the story. It begins with violence and ends with violence.
(b) The effective use of flashback in the early section. The opening paragraphs show us something happening, and we are then told how it has come about.
(c) Hans's reason for revisiting the farm, 'He didn't like to say that he wanted a little human friendship . . .' (I. 315), is very plausible and adds to the final tragedy.

Ein Weibchen: (*German*) a little woman
We'd better be getting on our way: We must leave
as thirsty as the devil: very thirsty

Willi was a good little chap, but soft: Willi was a good person, but was inclined to be too kind
had scuttled like rabbits: had hurriedly retreated
wouldn't meet him half-way: wouldn't compromise
hard as nails: unyielding
as sober as a judge: sober
C'est le premier pas qui coûte: (*French*) Only the beginning is difficult
knew the city like the palm of his hand: was very familiar with the city
He had a good bump of locality: He had a good sense of direction, a good memory for where he had been
Cochon: (*French*) Pig (abusive)
Bonjour, la compagnie: (*French*) Good day everyone
got on his nerves: irritated him
wolfed: eaten ravenously
moment his back was turned had set to with the others: as soon as he had left had started to eat with the others
got hold of: obtained
a lucky break: a piece of good fortune
made no headway with: did not improve his relationship with
had come round: had been persuaded
crying her eyes out: crying bitterly or profusely
going out of her mind: going insane
called to the colours: conscripted
Il faut souffrir: (*French*) It must be endured
Ich liebe dich: (*German*) I love you
war of '70: The war between France and Prussia in 1870
make a good thing: greatly improve
while you eat the fat of our land: while you take the best that we have. A biblical phrase. See Genesis 41
He hadn't had a bad education himself: He had received a rather good education himself
he couldn't hold a candle to her: he could not be compared with her
he was a Dutchman: he was deceiving himself. He was not recognising the obvious
easy-going: good natured, pleasant
he would have a pull: he would be able to influence
always ready to give a hand: always ready to help
she bit my head off: she spoke very angrily to me
let bygones be bygones: let us forget the past
if we play our cards well: if we are shrewd
That would be the last straw: short for 'That would be the last straw that breaks the camel's back' meaning that any more would prove intolerable
a by-blow: a bastard, or a child resulting from rape

Part 3
Commentary

The short story

Origins and history

The short story is a very old literary form. It probably originated with the religious stories of the Greeks, but it did not become widespread until the Middle Ages when collections such as the immortal tales of *The Arabian Nights* and Boccaccio's *Decameron* enjoyed a wide popularity. Throughout the Renaissance, in Italy, Spain, France, and England, there was a great vogue for brief narratives such as Cervantes' *Exemplary Tales*. In the eighteenth century, particularly in England, the short story was widely used as a vehicle for moral lessons. The rise of the novel saw the decline of the story. As public tastes changed, booksellers ceased to offer money for collections of tales, and authors came to look askance at a form that offered them neither cash nor credit. But at the beginning of the nineteenth century a new form of publication was put before the reading public which soon acquired an immense popularity. This was the annual. It originated in Germany. It consisted of a miscellany of verse and prose, and seems to have offered its readers a substantial fare, for Schiller's 'Maid of Orleans', and Goethe's 'Herman and Dorothea' were first published in annuals. English and American publishers were quick to see the potential of the annual and it was soon flourishing on both sides of the Atlantic. The annual was followed by the keepsake, and the keepsake by the monthly or weekly magazine. These publications created an enormous demand for short stories.

The two writers who have been most responsible for giving the short story its present shape are the Russian, Anton Chekhov (1860–1904), and the Frenchman, Guy de Maupassant (1850–93). Maugham has written extensively on both.

Chekhov

Chekhov is a master of the type of story which persuades the reader that he is not looking into a book but out on to a world. His influence has been considerably greater than Maupassant's, but he has proved much more difficult to imitate. His stories are generally wrought about a complex of emotions, and are as casual as the men and women in his four long plays. He avoids the unexpected and the dramatic, and shows scant regard for plot. As Richard Cordell has pointed out, irrelevant and sometimes wrong things are said in Chekhov's stories, inconsequential things are done, crises are approached and shunned, and the plot sometimes seems to end in the air. Chekhov himself claimed that he wanted to evoke a sense of reality rather than create an impression of realism, to capture a glimpse of the mysteries and perplexities of life rather than show a slice of life.

When Maugham read Chekhov, he discovered, as he said in *A Writer's Notebook*, a spirit vastly to his liking, one with whom he could 'get on terms of intimacy'. He was impressed by the way Chekhov pointed him away from art to life, the way he saw in his characters moments as well as men. They seemed to Maugham to be not persons but human beings, each one as it were a part of everyone else, and saved only from becoming shadowy and inconsequential by touches of idiosyncrasy. He was also attracted to Chekhov's affirmation of normality, and his clear insights into the sentimental mind that covers itself with deceit, smugness, and cant. But he was repelled by his formlessness. 'I do not know if I could ever have written stories in the Chekhov manner,' he wrote in *The Summing Up*. 'I did not want to. I wanted to write stories that proceeded, tightly knit, in an unbroken line from the exposition to the conclusion.'

Though Maugham was not influenced by the type of story that Chekhov wrote, he brought away from his study of the Russian writer a profound regard for his ironic detachment, his dignified reserve, and his scientific objectivity. This is not surprising as both trained as doctors, and both have emphasised in their writings that their study of medicine profoundly influenced the way they looked at the world. Whenever Maugham demonstrates a willingness to pose a problem and leave it at that, he is being essentially Chekhovian.

Maupassant

Maupassant is a master of the tightly constructed, crisp, narrative story, bare of inconsequential detail, that has a well defined beginning, middle, and end. Of all writers of the short story he is one of the most uncompromising. He presents the bitterest aspects of French life and French literature with the devastatingly quiet assumption that his point of view is the only one possible. He does not preach or moralise, praise or condemn; he simply presents. He sedulously avoids social and philosophical generalisations with the result that there is nothing to alleviate the stark particularity of his stories. There are none of the suggestive half-lights in his work that we find in Chekhov, nor any of those delicate nuances of tone that suggest the grey areas of life. Maupassant sees his favourite subjects, the peasant, the prostitute, the clerk, and the timid bourgeois, in an unpitying light that exposes their frayed collars, worn cuffs, and shrivelled souls.

In order to achieve the distance necessary for his chilly appraisal, Maupassant has put a large number of his stories into the mouth of a narrator. The form is admirably suited to his moral vision, for the narrator can suggest a man who has elected to stand on the perimeter of life, and whose chief interest is to recall proofs of its incoherence or cruelty and examples of its transitory pleasures.

By the time he was twenty, Maugham had read most of Maupassant's stories. Their lucidity, directness, and dramatic immediacy made a deep impression on him. Most of all he admired Maupassant's strong sense of form. 'His stories do not', he once wrote admiringly, 'wander along an uncertain line, so you cannot see where they are leading, but follow without hesitation, a bold and vigorous curve.' Maugham liked the way the settings were established with brevity and clarity, and the way the characters were described with just enough detail to make their role in the story plain. He noted with approval that Maupassant only used description to advance the plot, and that his characters, while strongly realised, were subordinate to the plot.

Many have criticised Maupassant for his deliberate artistry. His stories, they say, are too contrived. Maugham believed that this was not only admissible, but desirable. The writer does not aim at a transcription of life, he argued, but a dramatisation of it. Maupassant was correct when he arranged what he had seen and heard into a pattern, in order the better to interest, excite, or surprise. According to Maugham a writer should be willing to risk plausibility for effect; he should aim to tell his story so well that the reader does not notice that the raw material of the story has been carefully arranged.

It would be an injustice to call Maugham a disciple of Maupassant. He rather endorsed what Maupassant had achieved. His admiration for his work, and his defence of his technique, arose from affinities of outlook and temperament. There is the same pessimism, the same despairing assumptions about the quality of human relationships, especially those between the sexes. There is the same desire to write about the elemental passions, to describe the way convention is split by the dark forces of human nature; and there is the same desire to observe life, rather than to participate in it. Finally Maugham, like Maupassant, demands a certain type of response from his readers. He asks us to limit our expectations. There is room in the house of Chekhov for men of many philosophies; Maugham and Maupassant invite a select company of guests.

Maugham's theory of the short story

Maugham has written at length about his theory of the short story. He is fundamentally an exponent of the school of thought that it is the business of the writer of short stories to have a story to tell, and to tell it. 'As a writer of fiction,' he said in *The Summing Up*:

> I go back, through innumerable generations, to the teller of tales round the fire in the cavern that sheltered neolithic man. I have had some sort of story to tell and it has interested me to tell it. To me it has been a sufficient object in itself.   (*The Summing Up*, p.145)

Elsewhere he wrote:

> I have never pretended to be anything but a story-teller. I have little patience with those writers who preach or philosophise. I think it much better to leave philosophy to the philosophers, and social reform to the social reformers.

The sole business of the writer, Maugham thought, was to entertain.

He preferred the type of story that could be told over a dinner table, at a bar, or in a ship's smoking room. At its base is an anecdote; the narration of a single event, material or spiritual, which, by the elimination of everything that is not strictly relevant, has been given a dramatic unity. Many of Maugham's best stories can be readily summarised in a single sentence; 'Rain' for example: A missionary apparently reforms a prostitute, but he falls prey to her charms and commits suicide; or 'The Unconquered': a French girl who has been raped and made pregnant by a German soldier gets her revenge by drowning the child he has come to look forward to as soon as it is born.

The difficulty about basing a story on an anecdote is that an anecdote is a finished thing in itself. It is complete. The first time one is told an anecdote it pleases, the second time is likely to be trying, and the third is certain to be boring. Maugham believed that the best stories were those in which the anecdote had been expanded and given a definite shape. If this were accomplished successfully, the story could be read again and again for the cleverness with which it had been told. As he said in *A Writer's Notebook*:

> I wonder if the form of a story isn't a sort of memoria technica* that holds it in your memory. Why does one remember Guy de Maupassant's best stories ...? It is not only the anecdote. The anecdote is no better than in a thousand other stories one has read and forgotten. This reflection has been occasioned by a story of G's. ... The story was interesting and complicated; but it fell into two parts, each of

---

*memoria technica: a system used to assist memory.

> which would have made a good story, and he hadn't had the sense of form to combine them into a unity.
>
> I think you must make sure not to divide the interest in a story; Chekhov, however haphazard his sometimes appear, took care never to do this. In fact ... you must make up your mind what your point is and stick to it like grim death. That is just another way of saying that it must have form. (*A Writer's Notebook*, p.295)

Maugham strongly favoured the Aristotelian definition of form; that a plot should have a beginning, a middle, and an end. The beginning of a short story should set the scene with brevity and clarity, and introduce one or more of the main characters in such a way that the reader is supplied with sufficient information to accept their presence, and given some indication of the role that they are to play. These conditions are met, for example, in the introduction to 'The Facts of Life'.

> It was Henry Garnet's habit on leaving the city of an afternoon to drop in at his club and play bridge before going home to dinner. He was a pleasant man to play with. He knew the game well and you could be sure that he would make the best of his cards. He was a good loser; and when he won was more inclined to ascribe his success to his luck than to his skill. He was indulgent, and if his partner made a mistake could be trusted to find an excuse for him. It was surprising then on this occasion to hear him telling his partner with unnecessary sharpness that he had never seen a hand worse played . . . . (I. 219)

We are given enough detail about Henry Garnet to accept his presence in the story, and the sentence 'It was surprising then on this occasion . . .', tells us that it will be about what has upset him.

The beginning of a good short story should also arouse the reader's interest. Here are some examples of the opening sentences of Maugham's stories:

> When I was introduced to Lawson by Chaplin, the owner of the Hotel Metropole at Apia, I paid no particular attention to him. (I. 117)

We read on because we want to discover why the narrator did not pay much attention to someone who, it is implied, eventually proved interesting.

> A good many people were shocked when they read that Captain Forestier had met his death in a forest fire when trying to save his wife's dog, which had been accidentally shut up in the house. (I. 284)

This is an arresting opening because we are told the anecdote on which the story is based. It challenges us to find out who Captain Forestier was, why he risked his life for a dog, and why a good many people were shocked when they read about his death.

> One of the many inconveniences of real life is that it seldom gives you a complete story. (I. 353).

This plays on our curiosity. The implication is that what follows is exceptional.

The middle of the short story is the place where the writer, in Maugham's words, must 'stick to [the point] like grim death.' What he meant is that the writer must not introduce events which do not directly contribute to the unfolding of the action, and that he must restrict his description of character to those details that are relevant to the plot. The succession of incidents that make up the plot should follow one another in a strictly logical order. In 'Rain' for example, the reader is carried forward incident by incident to the conclusion. The opening paragraph introduces Dr Macphail, and sets the tone of the story. The next establishes the Davidson's prudishness. Then the conversation between Dr Macphail and Mrs Davidson, as the ship on which they are travelling comes into Pago-Pago, enlarges the reader's understanding of the Reverend Davidson's unsuccessful attempts to combat the immorality he sees everywhere about him. And so the story is skilfully built up, each incident growing out of and enlarging the previous one. All this time Maugham is sticking to the point; he is building up a picture of the Reverend Davidson's fixation on sex, and his lack of success in combating it. This one strand runs through the middle of the story. It grows naturally out of the introduction, and leads the reader inexorably to the conclusion.

Maugham considered the ending to be one of the most important parts of the short story. 'When the end is reached', he once said in a lecture, 'the whole story should have been told, and [the reader] should neither wish nor need to ask a further question.' The expectations that have been aroused should all be satisfied. Though curiosity may eventually lead us to wonder what happened to Miss Thompson and Mrs Davidson from 'Rain', this question should not come to our minds the first time we finish the story.

Maugham ends his stories in a variety of ways. Many end with suicide or death: 'The Pool', and 'Mackintosh'; several with clichés: 'The Facts of Life', and 'The Happy Couple'; some by a statement from the narrator: 'The Romantic Young Lady.'

> That was the end of the adventure. José León continued to drive the Countess de Marbella, but she noticed that when they sped up and down the Delicias that henceforward as many eyes were turned on her handsome coachman as on her latest hat; and a year later Pilar married the Marqués de San Esteban. (I. 362)

Generally speaking the ending returns the reader to the original point of the story. With 'The Voice of the Turtle' Maugham deliberately breaks the mood of La Falterona's rendition of Isolde's death-song to return the reader to the world of the narrator.

> La Falterona's voice, even now, was exquisite in quality, mellow and crystalline; and she sang with wonderful emotion, so tenderly, with such tragic, beautiful anguish that my heart melted within me. I had a most awkward lump in my throat when she finished, and looking at her I saw that tears were streaming down her face. I did not want to speak. She stood quite still looking out at that ageless sea.

Chekhov would probably have ended the story here, but Maugham insists on returning to the point: the way people see other people.

> What a strange woman! I thought then that I would sooner have her as she was, with her monstrous faults, than as Peter Melrose saw her, a pattern of all the virtues. But then people blame me because I rather like people who are a little worse than is reasonable. She was hateful, of course, but she was irresistible. (I. 284)

This ending emphasises what is best and what is worst in Maugham's theory of the short story. What is worst is its restrictiveness. By adding the final paragraph Maugham brings the reader up with a jolt and a cliché. Instead of floating out of the story, reflecting on the impossibility of coming to understand other people, the reader stops at the final description of La Falterona. What is best is its completeness. The final paragraph keeps 'The Voice of the Turtle' in the world of fiction, and persuades the reader that he has been entertained with a good story. Maugham believed that the latter, because it is difficult to achieve, was sufficient.

Special studies

Characterisation

Unlike longer forms of fiction, the short story does not allow a writer much space to develop his characters. Bound by a limit of several thousand words, he must content himself with showing how one or two aspects of personality undergo change, or are revealed as the result of a conflict. It is therefore necessary for him to establish the main traits of his principal character or characters as quickly and as economically as possible.

In 'Rain' for example, Maugham sets the scene and establishes Dr Macphail's character in the first paragraph.

> It was nearly bed-time and when they awoke next morning land would be in sight. Dr Macphail lit his pipe and, leaning over the rail,

searched the heavens for the Southern Cross. After two years at the front and a wound that had taken longer to heal than it should, he was glad to settle down quietly at Apia for twelve months at least, and he felt already better for the journey. Since some of the passengers were leaving the ship next day at Pago-Pago they had had a little dance that evening and in his ears hammered still the harsh notes of the mechanical piano. But the deck was quiet at last. A little way off he saw his wife in a long chair talking with the Davidsons, and he strolled over to her. When he sat down under the light and took off his hat you saw that he had very red hair, with a bald patch on the crown, and the red, freckled skin which accompanies red hair; he was a man of forty, thin, with a pinched face, precise and rather pedantic; and he spoke with a Scots accent in a very low, quiet voice. (I. 9)

This is skilful. We are given just the right amount of physical detail for us to 'see' Dr Macphail, and we are told enough about his background and his personality to visualise the type of person he is. What is significant, in terms of the plot, is that Maugham has established the tone of his point of view, for we see most of what happens through the eyes of Dr Macphail. The reader has to get to know the way he sees things as clearly and as quickly as possible. Maugham has chosen this point of view to achieve a particular effect. The passionate encounter between the missionary and the prostitute is best viewed by someone who is slightly reserved. We generally allow more to someone who under-emphasises rather than over-emphasises what has happened. In this way he secures the maximum dramatic impact for his story.

The crucial point that emerges from this example is that a character must add a dimension to the story. It is not enough for him simply to be there. In 'Rain' Dr Macphail's reserve provides an alternative to the Reverend Davidson's zeal, Miss Thompson's noisy familiarity, and his wife's and Mrs Davidson's hushed respectability. The type of emotional response that is associated with his personality significantly enriches the emotional pattern of the story.

Another very effective means of characterisation that Maugham employs involves the use of synecdoche: the use of a part to represent the whole. The personality of Annette Périer in 'The Unconquered' for example, is established through the changes in expression of her eyes. They look hard; they flash with anger; they burn with indignation; they gleam with terrible resolve; they darken with hatred. Apart from this we are not told very much about her appearance. We get odd details here and there: 'She wasn't very pretty' (I. 318), or 'that refinement which [Hans] couldn't account for, and those dark eyes, the long pale face—there was something intimidating about the girl.' (I. 315) That we are not given a detailed description of her person does not matter. By projecting her character through the expressions in her eyes, Maugham creates a vivid picture of that aspect of her being which is most relevant to the story. The eyes, as the proverb says, are the windows of the soul, and it is Annette's soul that has not been conquered.

The most common method of characterisation that Maugham employs is a detailed pen-portrait. It generally consists of a careful description of a character's physical appearance, and a brief account of the aspect of his personality that is important for the story. Many of these pen-portraits are based on people Maugham had met in his extensive travels. Wherever he went he took careful notes. In 1916, for example, he entered the following in one of his notebooks:

> Gardner is a German American who has changed his name from Kärtner, a fat, bald-headed, big man, always in very clean white ducks; he has a round, clean-shaven face and he looks at you benignly through gold-rimmed spectacles. The *faux bon homme*. He is here to open a business for a San Francisco firm of jobbers in the goods sold on the island, calicos, machinery, everything that is saleable, which they exchange for copra. He drinks heavily, and though fifty is always ready to stay up all night with the 'boys', but he never gets drunk. He is jolly and affable, but very shrewd; nothing interferes with his business, and his good fellowship is part of his stock in trade. He plays cards with the young men and gradually takes all their money from them. (*A Writer's Notebook*, p.111)

Most of this is used for the character of Miller in 'The Pool'.

> Miller was a German-American who had changed his name from Müller, a big man, fat and bald-headed, with a round, clean-shaven face. He wore large gold-rimmed spectacles, which gave him a benign look, and his ducks were always clean and white. He was a heavy drinker, invariably ready to stay up all night with the 'boys', but he never got drunk; he was jolly and affable, but very shrewd. Nothing interfered with his business; he represented a firm in San Francisco, jobbers in the goods sold in the islands, calico, machinery and what not; and his good-fellowship was part of his stock-in-trade. (I. 129-30)

Fortunately for Maugham, Gardner could be turned into Miller with the minimum of alteration and he had a character who fitted neatly into the scheme of his story. The description of Gardner not only suits the setting of 'The Pool', but his heavy drinking and his shrewdness tie in well with the plot. In 'The Pool' Miller is used to provide a contrast with Lawson; the man who can live successfully in the Tropics as opposed to the man who cannot. Miller controls his drinking; Lawson becomes an alcoholic. Miller's shrewdness at cards and in business reflects his shrewd approach to life. He is aware of the dangers of a mixed marriage, so he takes Ethel for a mistress. Lawson's marriage to Ethel is a complete failure; he turns to drink and then commits suicide.

Though he often drew heavily on the notes he had taken while he was travelling, Maugham was fond of pointing out that the writer does not merely reproduce a description of the people he has met. 'The writer does not copy his original,' he once wrote,

> he takes what he wants from them, a few traits that have caught his attention, a turn of mind that has fired his imagination, and therefrom constructs his character. He is not concerned whether it is a truthful likeness; he is concerned only to create a harmony convenient for his own purposes. (*The Summing Up*, p.141)

This is, of course, protesting too much, and under-rates his indebtedness. Nevertheless it demonstrates an important principle that is true for Maugham and for many other writers. The writer is someone who imposes order and design on the raw material of life. What he gets is a few loose threads which he weaves into a pleasing pattern, and it is the pattern rather than the threads which is ultimately important. That he borrows from life does not mean that he wants to make his stories life-like; he borrows to make his stories better, to give them an organic unity. As Maugham once explained in a *Preface* to a volume of his short stories:

> I write stories about people who have some singularity of character which suggests to me that they may be capable of behaving in such a way as to give me an idea that I can make use of, or about people who by some accident or another, accident of temperament, accident of environment, have been involved in unusual contingencies. (IV. 8)

Style

Maugham's style is one of the most distinctive characteristics of his writing. It is natural, fluent, simple, and colloquial. But it was not formed without difficulty. The sentence construction in some of his earliest writings, such as *Liza of Lambeth*, is sometimes surprisingly awkward:

> They were both of them rather stale and bedraggled after the day's outing; their fringes were ragged and untidily straying over their foreheads, their back hair, carelessly tied in a loose knot, fell over their necks and threatened completely to come down. (*Liza of Lambeth*, Ch. VI)

Sentences like this are exceptional in Maugham's mature writing. In 'Rain' for example, he describes Miss Thompson after she has received the news that she will not be able to stay in Samoa in simple, but effective sentences:

> She was sitting in a chair idly, neither reading nor sewing, staring in front of her. She wore her white dress and the large hat with the flowers on it. Macphail noticed that her skin was yellow and muddy under her powder, and her eyes were heavy. (I. 34)

The sentences in Maugham's short stories are usually short and rarely complex. The elements are generally joined by simple connectives, the most common being 'and' or 'but'. Relation is frequently displayed by semicolons rather than coordinate clauses. There are no rolling periods, measured phrases, or subordinate clauses to give the sentences weight and magnificence. The reader is rarely arrested by an unusual turn of phrase, a striking simile or metaphor, and there is never any attempt to surprise with extravagant vocabulary. Strong words are sedulously avoided. There are remarkably few adjectives. What he gets is a steady succession of familiar words in what seems a familiar order, which neither excites the emotions nor stimulates the imagination. The reader is made conscious of a clear, logical mind behind the passages of description whose main aim is to record simply and clearly what is before him. Maugham's style invariably leads straight into his subject matter.

Besides its evenness, the style has an informality which makes for unimpeded reading. As John Brophy has pointed out, Maugham is one of the few serious modern writers to make colloquialisms the substance of his narrative. He does not reserve them exclusively as, say, Evelyn Waugh does, for dialogue, where they can vividly establish the scene, the social setting, or the period, nor does he use them as Joyce does, to illuminate aspects of his characters. Instead, he incorporates them unashamedly into the body of what he has to say. Maugham has defended his use of colloquialisms in *The Summing Up*.

> One should write in the manner of one's period. The language is alive and constantly changing; to try to write like the authors of a distant past can only give rise to artificiality. I should not hesitate to use the common phrases of the day, knowing that their vogue was ephemeral, or slang, though aware that in ten years it might be incomprehensible, if they gave vividness and actuality. If the style has a classical form it can support the discreet use of phraseology that has only a local and temporary aptness. I should sooner a writer were vulgar than mincing; for life is vulgar, and it is life he seeks. (*The Summing Up*, p.32)

In Maugham's best writing the theory works well. Consider two descriptions of Miss Thompson from 'Rain':

> She passed with her nose in the air, a sulky look on her painted face, frowning, as though she did not see them. (I. 31)

The colloquial 'with her nose in the air' is cleverly associated with the unusual combination of a 'sulky look' on a 'painted face' to give a vivid picture of cheap hauteur.

> She slopped about her room, unkempt and dishevelled, in her tawdry dressing-gown. (I. 44)

The colloquial 'slopped about her room' is arrested by the more formal 'unkempt and dishevelled', and reinforced by the rich combination of the adjective 'tawdry', a word not commonly used, and the noun, 'dressing-gown'. In both sentences a colloquial expression has been skilfully juxtaposed with a more formal structure to produce a vital image.

Maugham frequently mixes colloquialisms and formal English with success in the short stories that are told by a narrator. The introduction to 'Appearance and Reality' provides an excellent example:

> I do not vouch for the truth of this story, but it was told me by a professor of French literature at an English university, and he was a man of too high a character, I think, to have told it to me unless it were true. His practice was to draw the attention of his students to three French writers who in his opinion combined the qualities that are the mainsprings of the French character. By reading them, he said, you could learn so much about the French people that, if he had the power, he would not trust such of our rulers as have to deal with the French nation to enter upon their offices till they had passed a pretty stiff examination on their works. They are Rabelais, with his *gauloiserie*, which may be described as the ribaldry that likes to call a spade something more than a bloody shovel; La Fontaine, with his *bons sens*, which is just horse sense; and finally Corneille, with his *panache*. This is translated in the dictionaries as the plume, the plume the knight of arms wore on his helmet, but metaphorically it seems to signify dignity and bravado, display and heroism, vainglory and pride. (I. 188)

The vividness and actuality of the colloquialisms like 'horse sense', and 'to call a spade something more than a bloody shovel' work against the stiffness of the formal structures to create a pleasing combination of calculated familiarity and cultured restraint. 'Good prose,' Maugham once wrote, 'should resemble the conversation of a well-bred man', and the best of his writing does.

The great danger with this approach to style is that it is too easy to slip from a colloquialism into a cliché. There is a point where informality ceases to be a means of expanding and vitalising language and becomes an end in itself. Maugham's novel *Then and Now* was bitterly attacked by the American writer and critic Edmund Wilson on this point: 'The language is such a tissue of clichés that one's wonder is finally aroused at the writer's ability to assemble so many.' Though this is severe, it is to some extent justified. Consider the climax of 'A Man from Glasgow':

> 'It was awful to hear it. A shiver passed through me and I cursed myself because I began to tremble. It wasn't like a human being at all. By Jove, I very nearly took to my heels and ran. I had to clench my teeth to force myself to stay. But I simply couldn't bring myself to turn the handle.' (I. 404)

This is not only poor English, but it is unworkable as short-story English. It is general and vague, and the short story demands language that is specific, alert, and allusive.

The question that poses itself is how Maugham's persistent use of the 'common phrases of the day' affects his ability to write short stories. Mixing colloquialisms and formal language is admirably suited to irony, dispassionate observation, the swift moving narrative, and the tolerant, common-sense, man-of-the-world point of view. The formal structures evoke the deeper emotions or suggest the complex ideas, while the colloquialisms provide the distance necessary for scrutiny. But it is not a technique that is of much use for describing strong emotions, specific settings, moods, or atmospheres. The colloquialisms tend to work against what is being attempted. They rob the moments of their significance and their individuality. On the other hand, nothing ages more quickly than the 'common phrases of the day'. Whereas in dialogue they may serve to vivify character and situation, they need to be placed with care if they are taken into the narrative of a piece of fiction, for they are apt to deaden the whole piece the moment they begin to decay.

Maugham frankly acknowledged his own limitations in *The Summing Up*:

> Poetic flights and the great imaginative sweep [are] beyond my powers. I could admire them in others as I could admire their far-fetched tropes and the unusual but suggestive language in which they clothed their thoughts, but my own invention never presented me with such embellishments; and I was tired of trying to do what did not come easily to me. On the other hand, I had an acute power of observation, and it seemed to me that I could see a great many things that other people missed. I could put down in clear terms what I saw. I had a logical sense, and if no great feeling for the richness and strangeness of words, at all events a lively appreciation of their sound.

> I knew that I should never write as well as I could wish, but I thought with pains I could arrive at writing as well as my natural defects allowed. On taking thought it seemed to me that I must aim at lucidity, simplicity, and euphony. I have put these three qualities in the order of importance I assigned to them. (*The Summing Up*, p.23)

To criticise a man who saw his own limitations so honestly for what he did not or could not achieve is pointless. Where style and subject are compatible, we must allow him success. His style is deft, urbane, natural, smooth, discreet, and eminently readable.

The Narrator

Most of Maugham's short stories are narrated by an imagined, unidentified speaker or persona who possesses a number of distinctive characteristics. He is above all a cosmopolitan. The social and geographical range of Maugham's work is remarkable, and the ease with which the narrator shifts from say a shabby hotel on Thursday Island to dinner at his London club helps to draw the reader into each story. 'The Pool' finds the persona sipping an early cocktail in the lounge of the Hotel Metropole in Apia. In 'The Voice of the Turtle' he goes to a literary sherry party in Bloomsbury where he meets a young writer whom he invites to be his house guest at his villa on the Mediterranean. 'A Friend in Need' finds him at the British Club in Yokohama; 'The Luncheon' in the Latin Quarter of Paris; 'The Human Element' at the Hotel Plaza in Rome. Because we are accustomed to seeing him in a variety of places we are never surprised when he talks to us from a new location. This of course is technically very useful. It allows Maugham at once to unify his work and enliven it with variety. What this type of narrator appeals to is our desire to escape. With him we can drink a gin pahit with a government official in Malaya, or swap gossip in a London club. As V.S. Prichett has said: 'Maugham gratified the wish to see oneself as worldly-wise and sagacious, to have impenetrable *savoir-faire*, to call for that dry martini and light a sceptical cigar at the end of the day.'

Much of this urbanity is established through the numerous digressions on wine, food, cigars, bridge, and other cultured pursuits that are written into many of the stories. Take for example the opening paragraph of 'Virtue':

> There are few things better than a good Havana. When I was young and very poor and smoked a cigar only when somebody gave me one, I determined that if I ever had money I would smoke a cigar every day after luncheon and dinner. This is the only resolution of my youth that I have kept. It is the only ambition I have achieved that has

never been embittered by disillusion. I like a cigar that is mild, but full-flavoured, neither so small that it is finished before you have become aware of it nor so large as to be irksome, rolled so that it draws without consciousness of effort on your part, with a leaf so firm that it doesn't become messy on your lips, and in such a condition that it keeps its savour to the very end.   (II. 171, 172)

From this exposition on the merits of a good cigar the narrator proceeds to the comparable pleasure of eating a dozen oysters with half a bottle of good white wine to the twists of fate that have been involved in their preparation and his enjoyment. Once the issue of fate has been introduced it is comparatively easy for the narrator to slip from the local scene to the human world of his story.

This is a skilful opening because, in addition to easing the reader into the story, it encourages him to relax. He feels assured that he is in excellent company. The narrator is a man of taste. He seems to understand the finer aspects of pleasure, so he is likely to tell a fascinating story.

Most of all we expect to be asked to observe rather than to participate. We expect to remain detached. We feel we shall be invited to observe a number of emotions, but we shall not be asked to experience those emotions through the lives of the characters in the story. Neither are we led to believe that what we shall be shown will be profoundly philosophical or emotionally harrowing. What we are promised is an hour of enjoyment. Many critics have slighted Maugham's stories which are told by a narrator, arguing that they are glib and slick, that they balance precariously on the edge of the commonplace, and that they skim the surface rather than plumb the depths. This is missing the point. The Maugham narrator is not a philosopher but a raconteur. If he did plumb the depths we should feel that he was speaking out of character and that the artistic unity of the story was being violated. The Maugham narrator is a man who can play a tolerable round of golf, a good game of bridge, and enjoys a hand of poker and a volume of detective stories. Though he can freely discuss many of the more obscure aspects of Eastern and Western mysticism, he readily confesses to being incapable of offering any penetrating insights into philosophy. He is essentially accomplished and cultured, a man who is as ready to play a game of bridge as he is to discuss the merits of the Racine alexandrine. When he offers us an interesting observation on Spanish literature or on Byronism, we are delighted to be taken into his confidence in this manner, but should he conjure up a Heathcliff figure or plunge us into the psychological turbulence of *Crime and Punishment* we should be disconcerted. Though he never stirs us profoundly he is never facile. His opinions and his judgements are sound, intelligent, and carry the imprimatur of wide experience. To criticise Maugham's narrator for not involving us deeply in his stories is like damning an apple for not being an orange.

When Maugham wanted to write a harrowing story he generally favoured the stance of one of the characters or adopted the point of view of the omniscient author. We see most of what happens in 'Rain' through the eyes of Dr Macphail, a reserved, precise, and rather pedantic man who is repelled by the excesses he is forced to witness. We spend most of the time in 'Mackintosh' observing what takes place from Mackintosh's point of view. In 'The Lion's Skin' we share the point of view of the omniscient author. We can survey past and present, read the characters' thoughts and see what has brought them together.

The one notable exception to the harrowing story told from the point of view of a character or the omniscient author is 'The Pool'. The history of Lawson's relationship with Ethel is hinted at by Chaplin, but largely recounted by the Maugham narrator, who, by the end of the story, witnesses for himself the confrontation between Miller and Lawson. Yet as readers we still tend to observe what happens rather than experience it because the narrator never surrenders his detachment. It is only towards the end of the story, when Lawson seeks him out, that he permits a degree of intimacy. While he listens patiently and compassionately, he remains objective, for when he retells the incident in the story he turns it into a generalisation:

> I held my breath, for to me there is nothing more awe-inspiring than when a man discovers to you the nakedness of his soul. Then you see that no one is so trivial or debased but that in him there is a spark of something to excite compassion. (I.151)

By focusing our attention on his attitude to the experience rather than the experience itself the narrator invites us to remain detached, to see Lawson as a type rather than an individual.

The willingness to listen that the Maugham persona displays in 'The Pool' is unusual. Generally speaking he finds such confessions distasteful. Maugham himself found people's confidences embarrassing. He wrote in *The Vagrant Mood*:

> I am either too self centred, or too diffident, or too reserved, or too shy to be on confidential terms with anyone I know at all well, and when on occasion a friend has opened his heart to me I have been too embarrassed to be of much help to him. Most people like to talk about themselves and when they tell me things that I should have thought they would prefer to keep to themselves, I am abashed. (p.196)

In 'The Human Element' the Maugham persona is shocked when the distressed Carruthers suddenly blurts out: 'I am so desperately unhappy', and then outraged when he begins to pour out his heart to him:

> It was amazing to me that a man so self-controlled, so urbane, accustomed to the usages of polite society, should break in upon a stranger with such a confession. I am naturally reticent. I should be ashamed, whatever I was suffering, to disclose my pain to another. I shivered. His weakness outraged me. (IV.359)

While he does not prevent Carruthers from telling his story, he treats his appeal for sympathy as an imposition, a claim for an emotional support he is reluctant to give.

By calling our attention to the tastes and feelings of the narrator, Maugham invites us to become a part of his world rather than the world of the story. We are invited to adopt a point of view, to accept a mode of perception. The dominant reality, as John Brophy has pointed out, belongs to the person of the narrator.

Accounts of the narrator's tastes in food, wine, women, cards, and ideas, and occasional revelations about his reactions to one or more of the characters, encourage this feeling of intimacy. When he confesses, as he sometimes does, that he does not understand a character, we allow the limitation because we have become accustomed to place our trust in his powers of observation rather than inquire into the motives of the characters for ourselves. In his account of the short story told in the first person singular in *Ten Novels and Their Authors*, Maugham states that 'the narrator begets in the reader the same sort of familiarity with the creatures of his invention that he has himself.' Clearly this familiarity is restricted, but we rarely feel its limitations. We rarely feel that we have been prevented from seeing or hearing something for ourselves that would increase our understanding. The narrator's obvious common sense, his tolerance, and his urbanity persuade us that we have access to everything that we can reasonably expect to know.

Sometimes Maugham exploits the amount of trust that he expects us to have in the narrator. He has the assurance to begin a story like this:

> I know this is an odd story. I don't understand it myself and if I have set it down in black and white it is only with the faint hope that when I have written it I may get a clearer view of it, or rather with the hope that some reader, better acquainted with human nature than I am, may offer me an explanation that will make it comprehensible to me. (IV.137)

This engages our curiosity and appeals to our vanity.

In the Preface to one of his volumes of short stories Maugham points out that the first person narrative has the merit from the story-teller's point of view that he need only tell his readers what he knows for a fact and can leave the rest to their imaginations. They can fill in what he doesn't or couldn't know. The writer must be careful that he doesn't write in long conversations that his narrator couldn't possibly have heard or include incidents which in the nature of things he couldn't possibly have witnessed. He must be careful not to sacrifice the great advantage of verisimilitude which writing in the first person offers. One of the principal objects of recounting a story in the first person singular is to achieve credibility. When someone tells us that what he says happened to himself we are more likely to believe that he is telling the truth than if he tells us something which is supposed to have happened to someone else. Personal experiences always seem more convincing than second-hand accounts.

Consistency and skill of narration are in fact the most attractive qualities of Maugham's narrator. We are prepared to surrender ourselves to him because we feel that what he is telling us he has witnessed for himself. Furthermore his restrained urbanity is appealing rather than demanding. He does not force us to listen to him. He captures our attention. As W.H. Auden once said: 'Readers, like friends, must not be shouted at or treated with brash familiarity.' Maugham's narrator wins our attention with his friendliness, he disarms us with his confidentiality.

In many places, particularly where he discusses art, literature, and ideas, the Maugham persona establishes a feeling of 'we' and 'they'. 'We' are the people of taste, discrimination, and above all, good sense, who are often irritated by 'they'—the professional critics, the slippered bookmen, and the academics who always seem to be unnecessarily intellectual. This appeal to common sense, in itself an inverted form of snobbery, is very attractive. It persuades us that we are sane, balanced, and cultured, that we are never needlessly critical, but that we know when and where to cast the suspecting glance.

Another appealing and distinctive characteristic of Maugham's narrator is his wry sense of humour. He is not above telling a story against himself. 'The Luncheon' sees him agreeing to dine with an admirer at a restaurant which he knows is far beyond his means, and then feigning loss of appetite while his guest eats her way through his next month's living allowance. 'The Poet', in which he mistakes the home of a bristle merchant for the house of one of Spain's greatest poets, and 'Raw Material', which concludes with the disconcerting discovery that the two men he thought were card-sharpers and whom he has been observing closely are really a pair of respectable business men—are both jokes at his own expense. This light-hearted self-deprecation endears the Maugham narrator to us.

Maugham is unrivalled for the range and richness of his stories told by a first person narrator. They are obviously amongst his best work, and there can be little doubt that they demonstrate what a skilful storyteller he is.

The exotic story

Many of Maugham's early stories are what are known as exotic stories. In his lecture on the short story to the Royal Society of Literature, Maugham cited Rudyard Kipling as the first to write this type of story:

> In his discovery of the exotic story [Kipling] opened a new and fruitful field to writers. This is the story the scene of which is set in some country little known to the majority of readers. It deals with the reactions upon the white man of his sojourn in an alien land and the effects which contacts with people of another race have upon him.

In writing about India and the Hill Stations in the foothills of the Himalayas, Kipling was writing from personal experience; he was born in India. Maugham's choice of the Pacific and the Far East was the result of a search for a new area of experience. His novel *Of Human Bondage*, he believed, had drained his subjective energies and exhausted his knowledge of the English setting. He felt the need around 1916 to discover a new source of material, a place where he could observe human life afresh. At that time he was working on a novel about an artist whose life was modelled on the life of Gauguin, and it was his search for more information about the rebel Frenchman that took him to the Pacific, where Gauguin's art had found its ultimate expression.

That Maugham should have selected a figure associated with the Pacific is not surprising. As early as 1904 he made one of the major characters of *The Merry-Go-Round*, say:

> My whole soul aches for the East ... I may not get an answer to the riddle of life out in the open world, but I shall get nearer to it than here. I can get nothing out of books and civilisation. I want to see life and death, and the passions, the virtues and vices of men face to face, uncovered.

In the same way Philip Carey, the hero of *Of Human Bondage*, longs to go to the East—to the Malay Archipelago, Siam, China, and the ports of Japan. He too believes that in an exotic country he will be able to get closer to the meanings of life. 'He did not know what he sought or what his journeys would bring. But he had a feeling that he would learn something about life and thus gain a clue to its mystery.'

That these characters were partly expressing Maugham's own wishes and opinions is apparent from an answer he gave to an American writer,

Robert van Gelder, who asked him why, after *Of Human Bondage*, he had so rarely returned to the English scene for his characters and background. 'In England civilisation goes fairly deep', Maugham replied,

> and it is an old civilisation. This makes for an apparent sameness in the people—one must go through many layers to discover what it is that sets each man apart, to discover the unique and the natural man. Each man is unique, of course, but the strangeness that makes a story, the oddity within him, is not so easy to find in a man who wears his civilisation so thickly . . . In those parts of the world where civilisation is worn thinner, I found the unique man far easier to see. Material leaped to me—I handled it as well as I could.

Maugham was particularly interested in the effect of the climate and the surroundings on the English people who had settled in the Tropics; the oppressive heat, the debilitating humidity, the sudden downpours of torrential rain, the ravaging forces of mould and rot, and the vast tracts of impenetrable jungle that remorselessly press in on the isolated outstations. In circumstances like these, Maugham observed, it was easy for a European to lose control of himself.

In a number of his stories the weather and the isolation are shown stripping away the thin veneer of civilisation that makes social intercourse possible. Mackintosh, for example, is driven to facilitate the murder of his superior officer by the oppressiveness of his environment, and the isolation that constantly throws them together.

> Mackintosh had slept badly and he looked with distaste at the paw-paw and the eggs and bacon which were set before him. The mosquitoes had been maddening that night; they flew about the net under which he slept in such numbers that their humming, pitiless and menacing, had the effect of a note, infinitely drawn out, played on a distant organ, and whenever he dozed off he awoke with a start in the belief that one had found its way into his curtains. It was so hot that he lay naked. He turned from side to side. And gradually the dull roar of the breakers on the reef, so unceasing and so regular that generally you did not hear it, grew distinct on his consciousness, its rhythm hammered on his tired nerves, and he held himself with clenched hands in the effort to bear it. The thought that nothing could stop that sound, for it would continue to all eternity, was almost impossible to bear, and, as though his strength were a match for the ruthless forces of nature, he had an insane impulse to do some violent thing. He felt he must cling to his self-control or he would go mad. And now, looking out of the window at the lagoon and the strip of foam which marked the reef, he shuddered with hatred of the brilliant

scene. The cloudless sky was like an inverted bowl that hemmed it
in. He lit his pipe and turned over the pile of Auckland papers that
had come over the Apia a few days before. The newest of them was
three weeks old. They gave an impression of incredible dullness.
(I. 155)

The pitiless hum of the mosquitoes, the ceaseless pounding of the surf, the stark brilliance of the scene, and the inescapable isolation fuel Mackintosh's hatred of his superior, so that he eventually loses control of himself and makes it possible for a disgruntled native to steal his revolver and shoot the man. Then Mackintosh himself commits suicide. The story recalls Joseph Conrad's 'An Outpost of Progress', but Maugham has drawn more convincing characters, and has evoked the influence of the environment more effectively.

Sometimes it is the location, rather than the climate, which exercises the greater influence on the way a character thinks and acts. The narrator of 'The Book Bag', for example, wonders if the setting of Featherstone's house, with the sharp contrast between the carefully tended gardens and the surrounding jungle, has affected the way he thinks.

I wondered whether, unbeknownst to him, the tender and yet strangely
sinister aspect of the scene, acting on his nerves and his loneliness,
imbued him with some mystical quality so that the life he led, the
life of capable administrator, the sportsman, and the good fellow, on
occasion seemed to him not quite real. (IV. 15)

As the story unfolds it becomes apparent that Featherstone has indeed witnessed a case of the dark, primitive passions that make the gentle, carefully organised society of the European community seem unreal.

Generally the pressures of life in the Tropics are made a contributing factor to the action. Only rarely does a critical point in the plot turn on the fact that a character has been changed by living in the East. In 'The Letter', for example, the defence lawyer's unethical conduct is directly attributed to the twenty years that he had spent in Malaya: 'He had lived in the East a long time and his sense of professional honour was not perhaps as acute as it had been ... He made up his mind to do something which he knew was unjustifiable.' (IV. 335) Though we would find it difficult to accept this type of behaviour from a prominent lawyer in the West or in a more civilised country, the exotic setting, which had been subtly evoked as one of the driving forces in the original crime, makes it easier for us to suspend our disbelief.

It is a tribute to Maugham's skill as a story-teller that he rarely yields to the temptation to use the Tropics as a *deus ex machina*. We are generally asked to believe that people act in a more extreme fashion in the Tropics, that greater demands are made on their self-control. We are only occasionally asked to accept the climate or the environment as the sole cause of a character's behaviour. The human element, whether it be sexual incompatibility, jealousy, excessive sensitivity, or a personality clash, is generally presented as the main motivating force behind the events of the plot. The exotic setting heightens rather than initiates the action.

The idea that life in the Tropics is at once more extreme and more precarious finds its expression in the titles of the first two major collections of Maugham's stories, *The Trembling of a Leaf*, and *The Casuarina Tree*. The first is from Sainte-Beuve: '*L'extrême félicité à peine séparée par une feuille tremblante de l'extrême désespoir, n'est-ce pas la vie?*' which suggests that the principal characters of the stories are unstable, that in their lives happiness and unhappiness are separated by so small a division or so slight an event that their situation can be compared to the trembling of a leaf. The title of the second collection was suggested by a tree that was introduced into the Tropics to protect the soil from erosion, and that has a grey untidy appearance that contrasts sharply with the lush tropical vegetation that constantly threatens to engulf it. To Maugham the casuarina tree symbolised the planters and administrators who, though they had brought a measure of stability to the colonies, would always remain obviously alien, and might eventually prove superfluous.

A number of Maugham's stories reveal his fascination with those men who had found ways of coping with the stresses of living alone in the Tropics. In 'The Outstation' he brings together a man who has come to terms with his situation and one who has not. It is a simple but powerful sketch of the antipathy that can develop into intense hatred when two people from totally different social and intellectual backgrounds are thrown together in a lonely place. Warburton, one of the principal characters, is the Resident of an isolated outstation in Malaya. Like the chief accountant whom Marlow meets at the coastal station in Joseph Conrad's *Heart of Darkness*, Warburton dresses immaculately to counter the potentially demoralising effects of his surroundings. He is snobbish, meticulous, and precise. Though he lives alone in the depths of the jungle he dresses for dinner, has a menu drawn up in French, at breakfast cuts and reads *The Times*, and corresponds regularly with the aristocracy with whom he once associated in England. He is a good administrator, and understands that the Malays have come to expect a certain mode of conduct from their colonial administrators. Cooper, the new assistant who is assigned to him and whose arrival opens the story, is his opposite. He is from a lower-middle-class colonial background, has vulgar tastes and manners, is careless in his language and dress, and despises what he sees as the pretentious complacency and self-assurance of the upper classes. Neither character monopolises our sympathies; we admire Cooper's down-to-earth approach as much as Warburton's obvious professionalism and his grasp of the Malay temperament. Shortly after he arrives Cooper begins to abuse the natives, and though Warburton remonstrates with him, hints at the possible consequences of his actions, and secretly tries to have him posted elsewhere, he persists with his insults. Finally he is killed by an outraged native. Warburton senses that Cooper will be killed, but he despises the man so much that he does not take any steps to prevent the murder. After the crime has been reported he instigates an official enquiry, for justice must be seen to be done, and apprehends the killer, who is punished in such a way that the Malays will realise that, while he does not condone murder, he understands that their code of honour has been violated. Once the whole matter is cleared up he resumes with satisfaction and thinly veiled relief the stuffy, formal routine which his unsuitable assistant had interrupted. Though neither Cooper nor Warburton is in harmony with their surroundings, Warburton has evolved such a distinctive way of life that he has been able to counter the potentially destructive forces of the jungle.

Though many of Maugham's stories dramatise the conflict between two Europeans, he was, like Kipling, interested in the problems of mixed marriages, and in the relationship between the Europeans and the half-castes.

Most of the mixed marriages in Maugham's short stories fail. The most striking example is the marriage between Lawson and Ethel in 'The Pool'. When the narrator first sees Lawson, he asks Chaplin:

'Is he often drunk?'
'Dead drunk, three or four days a week. It's the island done it, and Ethel'
'Who's Ethel?
'Ethel's his wife. Married a half-caste ... Took her away from here. Only thing to do. But she couldn't stand it, and now they're back again.' (I. 119)

Lawson begins drinking heavily to fortify himself against living in what amounts to a native manner. Soon after his marriage he finds his house filled with Ethel's relatives, Eurasians and natives, who no longer treat him with respect: 'His marriage had made him one of themselves and they called him Bertie. They put their arms through his and smacked him on the back.' (I. 130) As Lawson sinks lower and lower he comes to be despised by both the natives and the Europeans. In the end he realises that his marriage has been a mistake, that it has unleashed forces that he has not been able to cope with. 'I suppose I ought not to have married Ethel,' he confesses to the narrator. 'If I'd kept her it would be all right. But I did love her so.' (I. 151, 152) Miller, by contrast, who takes Ethel as a mistress, does not expose himself to familiarity from the Eurasians and the natives, and ostracism by the Europeans.

Maugham was strongly opposed, though not on moral grounds, to the mixed marriage. He believed that it was doomed to fail because of the cultural conflicts it unleashed, and because of the considerable prejudice it aroused in both the European and the native communities. A temporary liaison, as he realised from his travels, was often condoned, and could be the source of much happiness. Hutchinson, the English Resident in 'The Yellow Streak', attributes his happiness to his relationship with his native mistress. The danger came when a white man, who had been keeping a native mistress for some time, married a white woman. As soon as Guy's English wife in 'The Force of Circumstance' discovers that he has had three children by a native woman, she deserts him.

Maugham believed that the children produced by these liaisons were doomed to suffer. The half-castes, he observed, were despised by the Europeans, and rejected by the natives. Many believed that they had inherited the worst traits from both races. Even those half-castes such as Izzart in 'The Yellow Streak' who have attained high positions, are represented as unhappy creatures, at odds with themselves and the world, living in a twilight land that adjoins, but provides no access to, the European and the native communities.

The exotic story represents the work of a particular period in Maugham's life. It began when he went searching in the Pacific and the East for a new area of experience, and it ended when he felt that he could no longer benefit from foreign travel. In *The Summing Up* he has given an account of the impact he believed that this period had made on his life:

> I travelled because it amused me, and to get material that would be of use to me; it never occurred to me that my new experiences were having an effect on me, and it was not until long afterwards that I saw how they had formed my character. In contact with all these strange people I lost the smoothness that I had acquired ... [as] a man of letters ... I got back my jagged edges. I was at last myself ... I had sloughed the arrogance of culture. My mood was complete acceptance. I asked from nobody more than he could give me. I had learnt toleration. (*The Summing Up*, p.136)

The exotic story, for Maugham, not only launched him on his career as a short story writer, but it marked a significant phase in his personal development.

Part 4

Hints for study

What to look for in a short story

Here are some suggestions to help you in your study of Somerset Maugham's stories:

(a) First reading: Read the entire story, pencil in hand, in one sitting. Whenever you feel your interest flag, or you come to a section that does not seem to advance the action, make a mark in the margin. These will generally be the weakest parts of the story. Your first impressions are not infallible, but they are often a good guide.

(b) Make a note of the setting, and a list of the characters. Is it an exotic story? How is the setting related to the plot? Beside each character in your list write down the adjectives that are most frequently associated with him in the story. Study the relationships between the characters. How do they compliment one another? How are they contrasted with one another? What aspects of their personalities are most important for the plot? How does each character contribute to the emotional tone of the story? Where do the descriptions of the various characters come in the story? How effective are the characters? Does Maugham let them reveal themselves through their actions and their contact with the other characters in the story, or does he tell the reader about them? The character that reveals himself is generally more effective. Does any one character dominate the story at the expense of the others? Are all the characters appropriate to the setting and the plot of the story? Remember that Maugham generally presents characters in three ways:
  (*i*)   By emphasising one aspect of their appearance or personality.
  (*ii*) By having one character describe another.
  (*iii*) By the use of a pen-sketch; a short, detailed description of physical appearance and one or two traits of character.

(c) Write out a detailed synopsis of the plot. What is the chronology of the events that make up the plot? Do they follow one another in sequence, or is the reader shown something happening, and then given the background? This is called a 'flashback'. Does the story have 'a beginning, a middle, and an end'? If so, what are they? Now reduce your detailed synopsis of the plot to one or two sentences. This should be the 'anecdote' on which the story is based. Do all the events that make up the plot contribute to the development of the anecdote?

(d) From what point of view is the story written? The points of view most commonly employed are:
- (*i*) The omniscient author. This enables the writer to present the thoughts and feelings of his characters as well as the twists and turns of the plot.
- (*ii*) The point of view of a single character who is used by the writer as a central observer or a participant in the action. Often the writer selects a character whose personality harmonises with the tone that he wants to give to his story.
- (*iii*) The first person narrative in which the point of view is solely that of the character telling the story. What does the narrator tell us about himself? Should we believe everything he tells the reader, or should we be sceptical of his account?

Once you have ascertained the point of view from which the story has been written you will need to ask why that point of view was chosen.

(e) How does the story end? Re-examine the story to see how the reader has been prepared for the conclusion. If the ending is an unexpected one, a sting-in-the-tail, then is it effective? Does the ending bring the various elements of the story to a satisfactory conclusion?

(f) Language. Make a list of the images and metaphors associated with the various characters. What level of language has been employed—formal or colloquial? What effect does this have on the tone of the story? How, and to what effect, have the colloquialisms been deployed?

(g) Do you like the story? If so, why not? If not, why not?

Questions on individual stories by Maugham

(1) ' "Rain" is melodramatic rather than tragic'. How far would you agree with this criticism?

(2) Do you agree that 'The Fall of Edward Barnard' succeeds because Bateman's and Barnard's illusions are implicitly and not explicitly condemned?

(3) ' "The Pool" is marred by Maugham's failure to develop the main characters; Lawson's character is well drawn, but Ethel's is not.' Do you agree?

(4) 'The ending of "Mackintosh" lacks subtlety and truth of character'. Do you agree with this assessment?

(5) It has been said of 'Appearance and Reality' that it may have been 'too cleverly told'. What is your opinion?
(6) 'The three fat women of Antibes' has been called 'brilliantly ironic'. How apt is this description?
(7) How much of the success of 'The Voice of the Turtle' depends on the tone adopted by the narrator of the story?
(8) 'Although the characters and the events in "The Unconquered" are well drawn, the author's feelings, and consequently the reader's, are only superficially engaged.' How closely does this criticism describe your response to the story?
(9) How far would you agree that the character of La Cachirra in 'The Mother' is not developed sufficiently to make the story credible?
(10) ' "The Yellow Streak" is flawed; the reason for Izzart's behaviour is plausible, but the explanation of it is clumsy and unconvincing.' Do you agree?

General questions on Maugham's stories

(1) 'The contrast between the bitter, futile tragedies and the serene South Sea Island settings is effective.' (*Saturday Review*, 1921) Do you agree?
(2) 'In most of his short stories Maugham presents a dazzling picture from which he omits the human spirit; one begins the stories with excitement, but ends them disappointed.' (*Observer*, 1926) How far does this describe your response to the stories?
(3) 'Maugham's emphasis is too exclusively on fact and event; he should attempt some larger, more personal correlation'. (*Saturday Review*, 1926) Do you agree?
(4) 'Maugham's dexterity does not conceal the thinness of his themes'. (*New Statesman*, 1930) Do you agree?
(5) How far would you agree with the observation that Maugham's 'poise is both a triumph and a limitation'? (*Graphic*, 1930)

A suggested specimen answer to question (9)

How far would you agree that the character of La Cachirra in 'The Mother' is not developed sufficiently to make the story credible?

One of the problems facing the short story writer is that brevity can rob his characters, and hence his story, of credibility. In this regard it has been observed that the character of La Cachirra in Somerset Maugham's 'The Mother' has not been developed sufficiently to make the story credible. I do not agree. The events of the story are the outcome of La Cachirra's tormented isolation, her insane possessiveness, and her violent temper. These are all adequately explained. Her murdering Rosalia, whom she suspects of trying to rob her of her only genuine human relationship, is credible.

La Cachirra's isolation is the result of fear. She cuts herself off from the society of the tenement because she is afraid that the other residents will discover she is a murderess and will drive her out, as she had been driven out of her previous lodging. The residents who live in the tenement are afraid of her because she appears evil and menacing, seems obsessively secretive, and possesses a violent temper. That this mutual fear, which heightens as the character of La Cachirra unfolds, should provoke a confrontation is credible.

La Cachirra's insane possessiveness with regard to her son is also credible. She believes she has bought his freedom with the blood of the man who used to beat him, and with the seven years of imprisonment she has had to endure as a punishment for her crime. Having given so much, La Cachirra expects that her son's commitment to her will be comparable. When he does not respond to these unnatural demands she again commits murder to renew her claims on him.

Finally La Cachirra's violent temper renders her murder of Rosalia plausible. The young girl, who not only flaunts the youth and freedom which the older woman has lost, but who also taunts her and slights the sacrifice she has made, rouses La Cachirra's formidable temper.

Thus La Cachirra's character has been developed sufficiently to make her story credible. What seems surprising, and perhaps even improbable, is that Rosalia would wish to provoke such a tormented person.

Part 5
Suggestions for further reading

The text

MAUGHAM, W. SOMERSET: *Collected Short Stories*, Volume I, Pan Books, London, 1975

Other works by Maugham

MAUGHAM, W. SOMERSET: *Collected Short Stories*, Volumes II, III, IV, Pan Books, London, 1976
— *The Summing Up*, Pan Books, London, 1976
— *A Writer's Notebook*, Penguin Books, Harmondsworth, 1976

Books about Maugham

MAUGHAM, ROBIN: *Somerset and all the Maughams*, Penguin Books, Harmondsworth, 1975. Family history written by Maugham's nephew. Contains some interesting insights.
Conversations with Willie: Recollections of W. Somerset Maugham. W.H. Allen, London, 1978. A transcript of Maugham's conversations taken from notebooks kept by Lord Maugham. Covers the period 1945-65.
CALDER, ROBERT: *W. Somerset Maugham and the Quest for Freedom*, Heinemann, London, 1972. An excellent study of the novels and of Maugham's narrative technique.
CORDELL, RICHARD: *Somerset Maugham: A Biographical and Critical Study*, Heinemann, London, 1961. A good biographical section and some valuable analysis of Maugham's work.
CURTIS, ANTHONY: *The Pattern of Maugham: A Critical Portrait*, Hamish Hamilton, London, 1974. Uneven, but good on some aspects of Maugham's imaginative development.
KANIN, GARSON: *Remembering Mr Maugham*, Bantam Books, New York, 1973. Kanin was Maugham's Boswell from 1942 to 1954. A collection of random jottings, but fresh and interesting.

RAPHAEL, FREDERIC: *W. Somerset Maugham and his world*, Thames and Hudson, London, 1976. An excellent survey of Maugham's life and work. Lavishly illustrated. It gives a balanced estimate of the way Maugham's homosexuality affected his writing.

Other collections of short stories

CLINE, C.L. (Ed.): *The Rinehart Edition of Short Stories*, (Alternate Edition), Holt, Rinehart, and Winston, New York, 1964. This contains a good selection of short stories including Maupassant's 'Two Little Soldiers', Chekhov's 'The Lady with the Little Dog', Conrad's 'The Outpost of Progress', and Maugham's 'The Outstation'.

Books about the short story

O'CONNOR, FRANK: *The Lonely Voice: A Study of the Short Story*, Revised and enlarged edition, Bantam Books, New York, 1968.
O'FAOLAIN, SEAN: *The Short Story*, Mercier Press, Cork, Ireland, 1972. An excellent study of the short story.

The author of these notes

PETER KUCH is a graduate of St David's University College, Lampeter, Wales and of the University of Oxford. He is teaching Modern Literature at Avondale College, New South Wales, Australia.

He has lectured at Newbold College, Bracknell, England, and been a guest lecturer at the State University of New York Summer School in London. He is an assistant editor of the new edition of AE's (G.W. Russell's) *Collected Works*, has written various articles, and his book on the literary friendship of Yeats and AE is forthcoming.

YORK NOTES

The first 100 titles
available Autumn 1980

CHINUA ACHEBE	*Arrow of God *Things Fall Apart
JANE AUSTEN	Northanger Abbey *Pride and Prejudice *Sense and Sensibility
ROBERT BOLT	*A Man For All Seasons
CHARLOTTE BRONTË	*Jane Eyre
EMILY BRONTË	*Wuthering Heights
ALBERT CAMUS	*L'Etranger (The Outsider)
GEOFFREY CHAUCER	*Prologue to the Canterbury Tales The Franklin's Tale *The Knight's Tale The Nun's Priest's Tale The Pardoner's Tale
SIR ARTHUR CONAN DOYLE	The Hound of the Baskervilles
JOSEPH CONRAD	Nostromo
DANIEL DEFOE	Robinson Crusoe
CHARLES DICKENS	David Copperfield Great Expectations
GEORGE ELIOT	Adam Bede *Silas Marner The Mill on the Floss
T.S. ELIOT	The Waste Land
WILLIAM FAULKNER	As I Lay Dying
F. SCOTT FITZGERALD	The Great Gatsby
E.M. FORSTER	A Passage to India
ATHOL FUGARD	Selected Plays
MRS GASKELL	North and South

WILLIAM GOLDING	*Lord of the Flies*
OLIVER GOLDSMITH	*The Vicar of Wakefield*
THOMAS HARDY	*Jude the Obscure* **Tess of the D'Urbervilles* **The Mayor of Casterbridge* *The Return of the Native* **The Trumpet Major*
L.P. HARTLEY	*The Go-Between
ERNEST HEMINGWAY	**For Whom the Bell Tolls* *The Old Man and the Sea*
ANTHONY HOPE	**The Prisoner of Zenda*
RICHARD HUGHES	*A High Wind in Jamaica*
THOMAS HUGHES	*Tom Brown's Schooldays*
HENRIK IBSEN	**A Doll's House*
HENRY JAMES	**The Turn of the Screw*
BEN JONSON	*The Alchemist *Volpone*
D.H. LAWRENCE	*Sons and Lovers* *The Rainbow
HARPER LEE	**To Kill a Mocking-Bird*
SOMERSET MAUGHAM	*Selected Short Stories*
HERMAN MELVILLE	*Billy Budd* *Moby Dick
ARTHUR MILLER	**Death of a Salesman* *The Crucible*
JOHN MILTON	**Paradise Lost I & II*
SEAN O'CASEY	*Juno and the Paycock*
GEORGE ORWELL	*Animal Farm* **Nineteen Eighty Four*
JOHN OSBORNE	**Look Back in Anger*
HAROLD PINTER	**The Birthday Party*
J.D. SALINGER	*The Catcher in the Rye*
SIR WALTER SCOTT	*Ivanhoe *Quentin Durward*

List of titles · 79

WILLIAM SHAKESPEARE	*A Midsummer Night's Dream* **Antony and Cleopatra* *Coriolanus* *Cymbeline *Hamlet *Henry IV Part I *Henry V* *Julius Caesar* *King Lear* *Macbeth* *Much Ado About Nothing* *Othello *Richard II *Romeo and Juliet **The Merchant of Venice* *The Tempest **The Winter's Tale* *Troilus and Cressida* *Twelfth Night
GEORGE BERNARD SHAW	**Androcles and the Lion* *Arms and the Man* **Caesar and Cleopatra* *Pygmalion*
RICHARD BRINSLEY SHERIDAN	**The School for Scandal*
JOHN STEINBECK	*Of Mice and Men* *The Grapes of Wrath* *The Pearl
ROBERT LOUIS STEVENSON	*Kidnapped *Treasure Island*
JONATHAN SWIFT	*Gulliver's Travels*
W.M. THACKERAY	*Vanity Fair*
MARK TWAIN	*Huckleberry Finn* *Tom Sawyer
VOLTAIRE	*Candide
H.G. WELLS	**The History of Mr Polly* *The Invisible Man* **The War of the Worlds*
OSCAR WILDE	**The Importance of Being Earnest*